The Man Un

by

Linda Nissen Samuels

Flt Sgt Jack Nissenthall 916592

Chiselbury

Published by Chiselbury Publishing, a division of Woodstock
Leasor Limited
81 Dovercourt Road, London SE22 8UW

www.chiselbury.com

ISBN: 978-1-908291-84-4

Cover design by Miki Shaw – **www.mikishaw.com**

To

BASIL SAMUELS

with grateful thanks for his support and research,
without which this book could not have been written.

Contents

Acknowledgements

The author and publisher would like to thank the following people and organisations for permission to use copyright material in this book.

The family of Reginald V Jones to use the foreword he wrote for Jack's memoir written in 1963 and his letter to Jack.

Alan Godfrey Maps, for permission to use extracts from their Old Ordnance Survey Maps, sheet 51 Shoreditch 1914 and sheet 52 Bethnal Green & Bow 1894.

The Francis Frith Collection for permission to use the postcards

Nelson Publishing Canada, for permission to use the extract from creating Canada, a History 1914 to the Present, published originally by McGraw Hill.

Every attempt has been made to seek permission for copyright material used in this book. However, if we have inadvertently used copyright material without permission or acknowledgement we apologise and we will make the necessary corrections at the first opportunity.

In preparing this book, I am also grateful to the following people and organisations who have given me additional information and guided me.

Rachael Abbiss, Jennifer Bell, Ted Bell
Frank Bernard, Julius Bernard, Garry Bernard,
Clive Bettington, Ian Bloom, Dennis Burton, Jess
Conway[1], Savas Couvaras, Adam Farson, Ivor
Glazer, Joseph Hill, Mandy King, Barbara
Kinghorn, Stuart Leasor, Diane Levitin, Brian
Parrot, Basil Samuels, Elizabeth Scott, Kate
Thompson, Umi Sinha, Martin Sugarman,
Doron Swade and David Zimmerman

AJEX -The Association of Jewish Ex-Servicemen
and Women
Battle of Britain Bunker Museum
Bawdsey Radar Museum
Jewish Museum
The Society of Authors

My sincere thanks to Scott Fraser for the photographs of the remains of the radar station at Rosehearty, 2022. He is Allan Leel's grandson, the great-great-grandson of Mr and Mrs Buchan, with whom Jack was billeted at 37 Pitsligo Street, Rosehearty 1940-1941.

---

[1] Jess Conway, Archivist at Stratford Library, Newham.

Foreword

Linda and I first met in 2021 during discussions about an upcoming exhibition commemorating the 80th anniversary of Operation Jubilee (Dieppe Raid), which took place on 19 August 1942. The new displays would focus on personal stories from individuals that served in the air, on the ground and underground during the raid, and aimed to shed light on the lesser-known history of the operation. One of the most striking stories from Dieppe was the experiences of Jack Nissenthall, an RAF radar and electronics expert who carried out a top-secret mission gathering intelligence and disrupting German communications. His strength, stamina and skills were put to the test on that day and 80 years later, his daughter carefully reveals his story to highlight the significance of his work to the Allied war effort.

The historiography for Operation Jubilee contains varied conclusions about the raid, with many historians considering it an ill-fated venture. This book reaches beyond the traditional arguments and the broad narrative, and takes a personal look at the career of a talented Jewish engineer who survived a crucial mission in 1942 furnishing the Allies with important information.

Linda has devoted much time and patience in researching and writing this book and provides an honest account of her father's life. Much of the work comes from stories shared by Jack and his recollections about serving in the RAF. Using material from Jack's unpublished manuscript - *The Wizard War* - and letters he wrote to his wife, the book provides a fascinating insight into his life and experiences.

Linda did not serve in the military, so perhaps writes from a fresh perspective analysing the life of a special forces operative and loving family man. During his career, Jack's extraordinary actions went under the radar and now Linda is shining a light on her father's accomplishments in a new and interesting format.

Dr Rachael Abbiss
Principal Curator
The Battle of Britain Bunker
April 2022

Preface

My father Jack was an extraordinary man.

His wartime exploits, which were kept under wraps for over twenty-five years were excitingly revealed when I was thirteen years old.

It was only then I found out that in WW2 he was asked to go on a suicide raid to Dieppe to discover the secrets of German radar.

Up till then he had just been an extremely fit, lovable, funny and eccentric father to my brother and myself.

We knew he had been in the RAF and was a radar operator.

Little did I know that when he was twenty-two, he was asked to go on a mission, which meant almost certain death. He had agreed to have guns from a ten-man bodyguard from the Canadian South Saskatchewan Regiment trained on him. If he was wounded or risked capture, he would have been shot by his own side. He was also equipped with a green suicide pill.

I have used excerpts from my father's unpublished manuscript *The Wizard War*. Together with some of the 200 letters he wrote to my mother from 1940 -1945; these form the main part of the book. These have been supplemented by present-day contributions from people who knew him.

All quoted passages are indented. My voice is not.

Having married the love of his life, Dally, he emigrated to South Africa where my brother and I were born. My parents were then invited to become citizens of Canada.

He had an exciting life, adapting to the different

countries and working in cutting-edge technologies; three continents, three new technologies.

Two books have been written about his wartime experiences. *Green Beach* by James Leasor and *Winning the Radar War* by A W Cockerill.

This biography tells the whole story of his amazing life.

Foreword to my father's manuscript *The Wizard War*
Reginald V Jones, Britain's war time Assistant Director of Intelligence (Science).

The start of radio broadcasting in the nineteen twenties brought the electronic age into the ordinary home. The principles of constructing the simple receivers of those days were within the grasp of many who had received no instruction in science; and with a little effort any man could individually listen to the world with a receiver of his own making and - if he stretched to a transmitter – speak back. He could hold personal theories about the best way to make an aerial or a loudspeaker, sometimes out of profoundly domestic items and utensils, and he could usually find, in the curious phenomena of radio propagation, facts to support his theories, however, unorthodox these might be.

In this atmosphere, the radio amateur came into existence and the radio shop flourished. It was fortunate for us in Britain that they did; for they provided the reserve of radio amateurs and servicemen who so effectively kept our radar and signals equipment working in the Second World War.

Afterwards, our chief opponent in the radio war, General Martini (Director General of Signals of the German Air Force) told me how much he envied us this reserve. Hitler had banned amateur radio in Germany before the war because it might offer scope for anti-Nazi activities; he deprived himself of a band of men skilled in the improvisations that were necessary to keep electronic equipment in operation in the war.

Surprisingly little has been written about the men who kept our radio and radar equipment working. Although among the most skilled of jobs, it might not have appeared among the most dangerous. But it quite often was, particularly when the equipment was airborne or shipborne; and it sometimes involved the hottest of action. Harold Jordan won an immediate D.S.O. listening in front of a German night fighter for its radio transmissions, Eric Ackerman a G.M. for ninety flights over the German radar defences, and William Cox an M.M. for his gallantry at Bruneval. Like Cox, the author of this book Jack Nissenthall, was a Flight Sergeant Radio Mechanic in the Royal Air Force who had volunteered for an operation of unusual danger. The operation turned out to be the Dieppe Raid. One of my vivid memories is that of Flight Sergeant Nissenthall reporting his experiences to me immediately after the raid – ending with a quarter mile swim under fire to reach one of the departing ships – and his high tribute to the Canadians manning their last Bren gun on a rampart built from bodies of their dead comrades.

This book is therefore the personal story of a man who willingly went into the 'hard, savage clash' of Dieppe spurred by patriotism and enthusiasm for electronics, and knowing that if things went wrong –

which they did - he had a peculiarly slim chance of returning. That he did return was due to his great physical fitness, combined with the cheerful and resourceful courage that shows in this book. His own deeds speak for them themselves; but he has generously remembered mine 'with advantages'- I only wish that I had such a tale as his to tell.

Prof. R.V. Jones
Department of Natural Philosophy
University of Aberdeen
7 April 1966

The Man Under the Radar

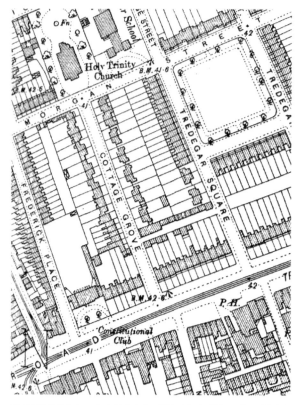

The Nissenthall family, Aaron, Annie, Marie, Jack and Michael, lived at 24 Cottage Grove, Mile End until 1926. Aaron's brother Max Nissenthall's fiancee's family lived at 12. Annie's uncle Joseph Fox lived and had a general store at 16 Coborn Road nearby.

Cottage Grove, Bow – an extract from 1894 Ordnance Survey. Number 24 is five houses in from Morgan Street on the right-hand side of the road.

Chapter One: Early years

I remember my paternal grandmother telling stories about my father, Jack, who was by all accounts an extraordinary child.

He was born 9 October 1919 at City of London Maternity Hospital, City Road, London. His parents Aaron and Annie Nissenthall married 11 September 1917 and shortly thereafter moved to Bow. The family lived in a big roomy house at 24 Cottage Grove, Bow, in the East End of London. It had a large garden, and is still there today, probably looking just as spruce as it ever was. Aaron's brother Max's wife's family, the Geetleman's were living across the road at 9 Cottage Grove. The houses are Regency in style and were constructed in 1823 to provide senior merchant seamen's families with accommodation befitting their status. Cottage Grove was close to the London docks in pleasant leafy, open surroundings and has since been renamed Rhondda Grove.

Jack's mother, my grandmother, said he never used the front door. When he came home from school, he would climb a tree and jump through his bedroom window. In *Green Beach*[2] he gets in by shinning up a drainpipe, going hand over hand along the roof edge, and jumping through the window. Whatever his method, Granny Annie, as she was known, said she always knew when he was home, because of the loud thump that announced his arrival.

---

[2] *Green Beach*, the book written by James Leasor is an account of Jack's wartime experiences.

24 Cottage Grove (now 24 Rhondda Grove) as it was; photograph taken in 2020. This is the house that Jack's family lived in until 1926.

Jack first attended Malmesbury Road School. He obviously liked school, because when his younger brother Mickey was 18 months, Jack took him there, riding on the family dog. He thought it was time Mickey should start learning.

My father told me himself that he remembered the

teachers saying Mickey was too young - he couldn't even talk yet. Unfazed, Jack told them that he could understand what Mickey was saying, and that he would interpret. They weren't convinced, and contacted his mother, who by this time was frantic, thinking Mickey had been kidnapped.

Apparently, Jack was also caught trying to set fire to the local park; I am not sure why. Probably it was some sort of experiment.

Jack's father, Aaron, was a successful master tailor. Aaron's older brother Max Nissenthall had brought Aaron out to England in 1909. Aaron trained as a tailor, specialising in ladies' clothes and eventually had his own business. On 11 September 1917 he married Annie Smietanski (who was also of Polish stock, but born in England). They had four children, Marie, Jack, Mickey and much later Harold. Aaron sounds to have been a bit of a character. Married, with children, he decided to keep a goat in the back garden of their house in Cottage Grove. The neighbours were not impressed. The goat was always escaping and destroying their back gardens.

Across the road was a "simcha" suite or banqueting hall which hosted grand events such as weddings and dances. One day the goat escaped, crossed Cottage Grove and interrupted a wedding by butting its own reflection in the decorative mirrors. That was the end of the goat.

Aaron was very proud of his adopted home. He was ever conscious of the freedom offered by the people of Great Britain. He encouraged his children to be proud English citizens.

Jack and his sister Marie. Photograph taken on the steps of 24 Cottage Grove.

After a few years in Bow the family fell on hard times.

The following newspaper article explains the catastrophic event which affected the family, and why Aaron and his family had to leave the lovely house in Cottage Grove, and move in with Annie's parents and brother Michael at 15 Blythe Street, Bethnal Green - a small, cramped house with a front door at the back of the footpath and just a very small back yard.

Aberdeen Press and Journal - Thursday 8 October 1925

"MOTOR BANDITS' DARING. Burglars Pose as Flying Squad Men. Motor bandits who posed as members of the Scotland Yard Flying Squad brought off a very daring raid in Merchant Street, Bow, London. Having forced open doors and ransacked rooms, they told a woman who protested that she was "under arrest." They locked a man in a room, and then drove off with dresses and materials valued at £1000. Two rooms of the house are rented by Mr A. Nissenthall for storing dresses, materials, and fancy goods, and it was this store which had attracted the attention of the motor bandits. Mrs Bentall, who occupies the house, told a reporter that she had just dressed with the intention of going to Wembley, when "I heard a knock at the door, at which I saw three men. They scarcely waited for me to answer, but forced their way into the house. After they had pushed me into a back room, one of them said—'Do not be alarmed. I am an inspector from Scotland Yard, and we are Flying Squad men. We are going to search for stolen property which we know is here, and we shall take it back to Scotland Yard!' He then began to cross-examine me like a detective out of an American crook play, until I felt like a criminal. Then he called to one of his men, and said— ' Get me a taxi-cab, sergeant. We shall have to take her to the station, and charge her with the others.' The inspector kept me in the kitchen while his assistants took the stuff from upstairs and loaded it into the lorry. "While this was going on, a friend of Mr Nissenthall arrived. The sergeant seized him, and, pushing him into the room, locked the door. He afterwards broke the window, and climbed through into the street. So ended one the most daring raids that have taken place in London." *[£1,000 in 1925 is equivalent to about £62,000 in 2020]*

My grandfather Aaron never recovered from this. The burglary broke him. It is presumed he must have had a 'nervous breakdown'. He took to gambling, and died of cancer in 1940.

Living now in Blythe Street, Jack and his two siblings, Marie and Mickey then attended Teesdale Street School. It was in the next street (easily accessible via a small road, Wear Street). At 15 Blythe Street at the time were Annie's parents Hersch and Augusta Smietanski, and Annie's brother Michael. At 39 Teesdale Street, lived the Bernards. Isaac and Mina were a Romanian/Yiddish speaking couple, who had 6 children; Victor, Max, Adelaide, (affectionately known as Dally) Maurice, Julius and Frankie. This house became Marie and Jack's home from home. It was a warm, somewhat chaotic, traditional three-story East End Jewish house, with a tailor's workroom on the top floor and accommodation for the five boys, one girl and their parents on the floors below.

Extract from the Ordnance Survey map of 1914. Jack's family lived at 15 Blythe Street and Dell's family at 39 Teesdale Street, both houses close to Wear Street. Jack and Dell both attended Teesdale Street School until they were eleven and then Mansford Street School, which is opposite the Unitarian Church.

Sadly the houses Jack knew in his childhood are no longer standing. Deemed unfit for human habitation, many of the houses in both roads were demolished to make way for new Local Authority housing estates. The two roads, or at least what is left of them, are now part of The Old Bethnal Green Road Conservation Area which was designated in October 2008. The Winkley Estate, which forms the major part of the Old Bethnal Green Road Conservation Area, is a small area of distinctive late Victorian development which now stands surrounded by post war local authority housing development. The houses in it are of the same style as those that used to stand in Teesdale Street and Blythe Street.

Jack in Wear Street, which linked Blythe Street and Teesdale Street in 1927.

There, when he was nine, Jack was introduced to electronics by his future double brother-in-law, Max, in a cupboard under the stairs. I say 'double', because Jack eventually married Max's sister, Dally and Jack's sister Marie married Max.

Jack, aged 9, started making crystal (radio) sets for the neighbours. He remembered how one not so generous neighbour gave him half an apple as payment; he was not impressed. Always very short of money as a consequence of the family's precarious finances, but with a great thirst for knowledge, in the holidays he would walk from the East End to the Science Museum in Kensington. He told me that for lunch he would eat fish and chips out of newspaper in the tunnel leading to the Underground, and then return for an afternoon session, before walking home again.

From the age of twelve, Jack and his friend Max Bernard would cycle to Whitstable on one bike, each taking turns to sit on the handlebars while the other pedalled. (Jack had family in the area, Bertha and Dick, whom they visited frequently). Later on they went camping at Box Hill with the girls in the family, and other friends. They also went to the Isle of Wight. The boys cycled, and the girls would go by train.

Jack with his father Aaron at Ramsgate

After he left Teesdale Street School in 1930, he went to Mansford Street Central School, which was essentially a technical college. There he was blessed to have an inspirational science teacher A.H. Raines, and it was he who probably set him on course for his future career, starting with a one-valve radio and then he went on to construct receivers under his guidance.

Jack was always looking for components for his 'hobby' and one day he cycled across London to the Columbia Gramophone Company shop in Petty France where he met a man called Alan Blumlein[3].

Alan was obviously impressed by Jack's

---

[3] Alan Dower Blumlein, 1903 - 1942, was an English electronics engineer. He was considered the twentieth century Faraday, with 128 patents for his inventions in telecommunications, sound recording, stereophonic sound, television and Radar.

enthusiasm, for, at Jack's request, and despite a heavy work schedule of his own, he agreed to give a talk to the Chiswick Radio Club of which Jack was a member.

In 1931, The Columbia Gramophone Company was bought out and combined with other similar establishments to form EMI. A brand-new factory with laboratories was built at Hayes in West London and Alan Blumlein went to work there.

In 1935 aged sixteen, Jack started working at EMI. Perhaps it was Alan Blumlein who persuaded him to apply, for Jack found himself working with Alan on sound reproduction, radio and early television. Jack assembled television sets and visited people's homes to install and maintain them. On 2 November 1936 the BBC Television, as it was then known, began broadcasting regularly from Alexandra Palace to the London area.

Of this happy time, my father wrote in *The Wizard War* manuscript:

> In those sunny far-off days it was quite unthinkable that anybody in the world would have the audacity to attack the British Isles. The First World War, the Great War, had been virtually forgotten. The victorious armies of Britain, France and America together with all the Allies had fought and won the 'war to end all wars'. It was now ancient history. Nobody would ever dare to attack Britain.

> In London, I was a tiny cog in the radio industry. Repairing and building radio and television sets, we strove to keep the

demanding customers happy. To further my education I attended, for three evenings a week, the Regent Street Polytechnic in the West End of London, that magnificent institution founded by Sir Quentin Hogg. My regular evening studies were at times supplemented by the bonus of short lecture courses by visiting scientific 'celebrities'. It was during one of these lecture courses that the mysteries of the cathode ray tube, then a new industrial device, were so skilfully unfolded [expounded] in great detail, by Mr A. G. Parr. His brilliant lectures not only prepared me for my daily work in television, but what was more important, for the trying time ahead in radar.

I had long since known that my life would be hopelessly bound up with the new electronic science. Late night hours spent in study were always gratifying as I felt I was continually expanding my ability to do the work I most enjoyed. I was extremely happy as my work was also my hobby, which enabled me to build devices that made me the envy of my friends. I had a most magnificent record player, a large-screen television set and I could tune in and listen, almost at will, to radio stations in practically any part of the world.

Life at that time for most teenagers was very pleasant. The Depression of the early thirties had long since passed and the young were becoming affluent. During weekends bicycle club members swarmed over the countryside.

Television, sport and the stage shows with artists like Lupino Lane and Jesse Matthews, made life for both young and old all over Britain more than easily bearable. Since the end of the First World War there had been mild war scares in various parts of the world, but no particular pattern of direct danger to England and her way of life ever developed.

We all felt concerned at the way Mussolini, using mustard gas, had deployed his military to suppress the Abyssinians and, by contemptuously ignoring sanctions imposed, had caused the downfall of the League of Nations. That one man could be responsible for the break-up of such a world body did not seem to augur well for the future. In 1936, the Spanish War had started and was used to promote the experiments in military hardware of both Mussolini and Hitler. At Guernica in Spain, Hitler had demonstrated to the world the effectiveness of his new-born Luftwaffe, his flying artillery which demolished a town and all its inhabitants in a matter of hours. This was his first demonstration of Blitzkrieg, 'Lightning War' and its threat of things to come was there for all but the blind to see.

At a political meeting, my friends and I had listened to Churchill's dire warning on the menace posed by the evolving massive German Air Force. Despite the obvious warnings of Manchuria, Abyssinia and Guernica, the danger to Britain seemed somewhat remote. Hitler had been in charge for about three years and we in England expected that, like all other continental crackpots, he would eventually fall from power. To the average Britisher this was the time to carry on with the football pools rather than worry about distant dictators.

My friends and I as a group had attended Churchill's meeting whilst camping at Stones Farm near Waltham Abbey, a pretty camping site in Epping Forest on the eastern outskirts of London. As young dissidents, we had attended the Conservative Party meeting with the express intention of having fun and arguing with the speaker. However, after a short exposure to Churchill's oratory, we found ourselves clapping, rather than heckling. His forecasts about the gangster Hitler and his Nazi tribe, left us all in little doubt as to what might transpire if something were not done to hold off the tyrant's march to [greater] power. He exhorted his listeners to help in his campaign against the new terror that was arising on the Continent. After the meeting I found myself wondering what I could possibly do to help in the defence of England if this madman did one day threaten us with attack.

I decided to learn as much as possible about radio and electronics and their potential application in the field of National Defence, realising that I could only be a very small cog in the defensive machine. Little did I then know that I, and a comparatively small group of other young radio men were, by sheer hard work, to become of vital importance in the development of Britain's defence system, already on the drawing board, but sadly starved of personnel. Furthermore, that I myself, would be forced into a predicament [a scenario] where my capture alive by the Germans, might have seriously affected our chances of surviving the war, as yet years away.

For we young Cockneys, it was just as well we did not know what the future held. Some three years later, my friend George Smith [a resident of Teesdale Street], together with most of his family were to die in an air raid on London. Tommy Baxter [another good friend], for all his Bolshie talk, loved his country and was lost with the *Rawalpindi*, making naval history when the light merchant cruiser deliberately, and with no support, challenged the mighty German pocket battleship, the Graf Spee in the defence of an Atlantic convoy.

Since I had first been able to wield a pair of scissors, I had become an avid model aircraft builder, my father's factory [tailoring workshop] ceiling displaying quite an array of my constructions. These consisted in the main of biplanes and triplanes, both German and English, which had achieved fame in The First World War. Aeroplanes and flying had always thrilled me and once I had received my first bicycle, I never missed an opportunity of attending an air display providing it was within cycling range.

Each year there was a local air display at Hendon. This was a high point which I never missed. On Empire Air Days I cycled out, usually to the beautiful aerodrome at Biggin Hill. There were also odd, but excellent shows like the 1937 *Daily Express* air display at the then small civilian aerodrome at Gatwick, near Redhill. Lord Beaverbrook, his son later to become an ace pilot, had offered a prize for the best aerobatic exhibition. This was a considerable amount of money and attracted pilots from all over the Continent as well as America. An extremely high-powered biplane flown by an American, Al Brown, gave a wonderful demonstration of high-power manoeuvres. French and Belgian pilots also gave brilliant performances. The RAF however, stole the show by cavorting all over the sky in an amazing series of aerobatics with their aircraft tied together wingtip to wingtip.

Despite the international attendance there were no flyers from Germany, which rather disappointed the enthusiasts who had heard so much of German flying skills. For me this was a great day as I managed to speak for quite a time to the two great Generals Erhard Milch and Ernst Udet of the Luftwaffe.

A disarming man, Udet was insistent that every young man of sound eye and limb should learn to fly. This seemed almost an obsession as he described the methods being used in Germany to train pilots. Since this was some three years before the outbreak of war, it all sounded innocent enough. General Udet, I am sure, was an idealist and I'm quite certain that this unfortunate man had no idea to what use his carefully nurtured brainchild was to be put. He had no thought of the fire and terror that they were to rain down from the skies on the peoples of Europe. General Udet committed suicide in 1941. General Milch became the supreme architect of the Luftwaffe who fought a losing battle against Hitler and his foibles.

In England it was Empire Air Day, in Germany, Adler (or Eagle) Day, the ultimate target was air proficiency to the nations of Europe that, from 1936 onwards strove to get their youth air-minded. This was particularly true in Britain where 1936 marked the beginning of the nagging doubt as to what would happen if the Nazi Air Fleet turned hostile and did try to attack.

What, in any case, were the requirements of an air defence system? First, a high-speed well-armed aeroplane to act as a fighter. Britain had just won the Schneider Trophy for high-speed aircraft for the third year running, which entitled her to retain the trophy. The machine, which for three years had outclassed all comers was a Super Marine S.6B using a Rolls-Royce in-line engine. Though a float plane, if fitted with wheels, it bore a strong resemblance to the Spitfire, as yet unborn. In typical British manner, once the Schneider Trophy had been finally won, apart from a few farsighted individuals, all interest in the prototype high-speed aircraft lapsed. Nevertheless, the embryo high-performance fighter aircraft had been developed.

After the weapon, the second requirement was for pilots and groundcrew. The RAF stimulated interest among the young people by holding open days for the public and these regular invitations did indeed do much to arouse interest in aircraft problems both on the ground and in the air.

Henry Tizard, [a chemist, who oversaw the development of Radar before and during WW2] however, realised that it would be no advantage to have excellent aircraft and would-be bomber pilots, if, when enemy aircraft came, they could not be located in the cloud that invariably shrouded the mist-prone British Isles. This, then, was the most difficult problem. A device was needed to detect the approaching bombers and a highly organised ground system had to be evolved to plot them accurately wherever and whenever they appeared. Once the attacking enemy had been located, then the ground stations could direct the high speed fighter squadrons to intercept them.

For this hitherto undreamt of project, Tizard chose Dr Robert Watson-Watt, a brilliant practical scientist, who had for some years been working on complex radio problems in connection with the ionosphere. (The ionosphere are the invisible reflecting layers above the earth which allow or prevent radio communications to distant parts of the world.)

If these three requirements, high speed aircraft, skilled pilots and ground control - could be met, then it might be possible to defend Britain against attack from enemy airforces. Watson-Watt, faced with the problems of developing this complex machine, had first of all to choose a site from which to conduct his experiments. To avoid wasting our RAF engine and pilot hours, he had to find a spot on the coast near which the international airlines flew on their daily schedules. After careful consideration, a site he had been offered near Felixstowe [at Orfordness] was accepted. From here the aircraft flying from Croydon [early Gatwick] out to the Continent could be used as targets for the experiments which were about to begin. [This original site was too exposed to the North Sea and somewhat remote. More personnel were required and larger premises for them to work in and live had to be found.] Bawdsey Manor[4], situated at the mouth of the River Deben in Suffolk was purchased by the Ministry of Defence and it would become the

_____

[4] This easily understood explanation of quite a complex subject is well worth reading. John Hearfield's 2012 essay 'Chain Home and the Cavity Magnetron' about the birth and development of radar is to be found on this webpage:
http://www.johnhearfield.com/Radar/Magnetron.htm

first Radar or RDF [Range and Direction Finding] station in Britain, as it was called in those days.

From 1936 until the outbreak of war in the autumn of 1939, small groups of men laboured tirelessly at Bawdsey under comparatively difficult conditions to produce the devices that would enable Britain, by the skin of her teeth, to stay in the war. People like Dr [Edward George 'Taffy'] Bowen and Dr [William Alan Stewart] Butement, worked virtually without respite, evenings, weekends and holidays. They originated the most amazing ideas and made them work in practice. It is sad to see how, as the years went by, these people, whose wonderful work and whose problems [converting radio waves into plots to range, direction and elevation] could not be understood by lesser men, were carefully pushed to one side. Most showed their feelings by leaving Britain forever, vowing never to return.

[Both Bowen and Butement went first to America and subsequently Australia.]

The critical period was 1937 to 1938, the appeasement era, during which the seeds of The Second World War were carefully sown. I followed the news carefully and noted how the British people's apathy and then fear followed a pattern dictated from month to month by Hitler and his gang. There were regular crises with Hitler insisting that his latest bit of burglary [annexations] would be his last, and after each crisis the peace-loving British people breathed a sigh of relief and went back to their pubs, their football pools and their racing papers.

During this period the people of Britain slumbered on, and hoped that the dictators, given enough rope, would hang themselves. To imagine Great Britain under attack by foreigners was quite ridiculous, too ridiculous to contemplate. The lone voice of Churchill tried to warn of impending disaster, but even he was derided by members of his own party. The British man in the street was convinced that the rest of the world was very much as he was, a balanced thinker with a reasonable liberal education and nothing but goodwill towards all the other peoples of the world.

My own thoughts were constantly focused on the question of what I could possibly do if Churchill was right and our little island were attacked. On one of my camping expeditions to Stones Farm, I plucked up courage and cycled through Epping Forest to the RAF aerodrome at North Weald (which in some three years' time was to feature as a star performer in the Battle of Britain). The men there were fairly friendly, but extremely security conscious. After one or two visits on succeeding weekends I was shown some RAF wireless equipment supposedly in use when required. I was shocked at the appearance of the vintage apparatus - it looked as if it had come out of the Ark. But who was I to judge?

I became friendly with an ex-Royal Flying Corps airman LAC [Leading Aircraftman] Bill Powell and he, with no lack of suitable adjectives, left me in no doubt as to how he felt about the RAF and its deficiencies, imaginary or otherwise. When it came to the test this type of man was imperturbable, untiring and unbeatable. His stories of The First World War, true or false, held me enthralled and I feel the great regard I developed and still have for the RAF all stems from his superb storytelling.

At work I chanced to meet a visiting RAF officer in civilian clothes, who was canvassing for men with a knowledge of television who were prepared to spend short periods working for the Air Ministry on a more or less voluntary basis. With a world so full of absorbing distractions by way of entertainment and most things being measured by the universal yardstick of pounds, shillings and pence, he was finding it more than difficult to enrol assistants. Sometime later I met him at a radio club meeting in Chiswick and, after further discussions, decided to go along with him and help in any way I could. It was all very haphazard and for a month or two nothing happened.

However, one Saturday morning after a series of telephone calls, I found myself travelling, along with two other men, north east out of London on the road to Felixstowe in a rather battered Fiat Cub. The 70 mile trip seemed interminable. I had compressed myself into the rear of this tiny car and I found it more than difficult trying to unfold myself when we eventually stopped at a roadside pub for some lunch. Here I had to admit rather shyly that I never drunk beer! Lunch was mainly dictated by our limited spending power and consisted of bread, cheese, beer and pickles. During the second part of our journey to the coast this repast played havoc with the internal atmosphere of the little car!

After skirting Ipswich we travelled towards Felixstowe, where we turned off and made for our destination, the location of which our driver appeared to know and about which he steadfastly refused to talk. Eventually we arrived at what looked like a towered country mansion set in beautiful riverside grounds. We were greeted by a middle-aged man, a security guard, who made us state our business. After a few words with the driver, who showed him our letter of introduction, with no further formalities he directed us along the drive.

Leaving us standing at the front door, our driver disappeared inside. After what seemed like an endless wait, he reappeared looking little the wiser for his visit. A further delay then ensued until one Sergeant Airey with his broken nose and a loud voice, appeared and lectured us at length on the need for security, and made us promise not to discuss any details of anything we did or saw while working in this establishment. Needless to say, I was very thrilled by the cloak and dagger atmosphere, and prepared myself mentally to honour at all times, even unto death, the assurances I had given. We would learn that beneath Sergeant Airey's rough exterior and foghorn voice, there was a very warm and helpful personality. For a short time and under his guidance we wandered around heavily battered by a boisterous wind that swept in from the sea. After he had had enough of the wind he left us to our own devices. There were a number of huts in the vicinity but very few people; there was certainly nothing that seem to be remotely secret around us.

Being more or less at a loss as to what to do, we hovered near a small group of men who were wrestling with a large pile of wooden spars which, Meccano style, they were trying to piece together. We offered our assistance and worked away for some two hours until we were finally rewarded with a rather wobbly structure some 15 feet high. Two older men came out to inspect our efforts, congratulated us all on our excellent work and, moreover, suggested that we all retire to the big house for some well earned tea.

In a fairly large room which functioned as a sort of communal dining hall, the staff sat drinking and talking. Self-consciously we entered and received what we thought were some strange looks from the 'natives'. We were looking very windswept and dishevelled but were quickly made to feel at home. After showing all and sundry our cuts and splinters from the mast erection, we were chided by some of the residents and welcomed into the clan.

Bawdsey, at the age of seventeen, became part of my father's normal life. Most weekends he would cycle the seventy miles on a bicycle with no gears, or take the train to Bawdsey Manor, never telling a soul where he was actually going. He always had been a keen cyclist and his family understandably thought he was doing his 'usual thing' of cycling around the countryside and camping somewhere over the weekend. He continues….

We soon learned that like us some of them had been voluntarily enrolled from trade and industry to assist in building small electronic units or other devices as they were required or even, if needs be, to help the fitters and riggers erect structures. They assured us that there was always something to do and judging by the spontaneous, enthusiastic spirit of these men, we knew we would all enjoy any task however menial.

Bawdsey became the first of what were to become known as CH stations. Each Chain Home consisted of four 350ft tall steel towers and three 240ft wooden towers. The steel towers were the transmitter antenna set out in a line 180ft apart. The wooden towers were for the receivers and were arranged in a square. Regardless of the weather or the time of day, if a fault was detected, someone had to climb up, find the problem and sort it out. Nobody had heard of health and safety.

Chain Home steel transmitter tower at Bawdsey, Suffolk. It is 360 feet (110 m) tall. It is taller than the Big Ben tower, which is 315 feet (96 m). In all sorts of weather, and sometimes in the dark, men used to climb up the ladder to service the transmitters. By comparison a CHL (Chain Home Low) aerial array was 40 feet (12.2m) wide and 20 feet (6.1m) high. The RDF station at Rosehearty was a CHL station. The transmitter hut and receiver hut had an aerial array each, both of which could be manually rotated to point in the same direction.

To save money I usually cycled out from London and camped near Bawdsey. This enabled me to enjoy a weekend camping, and at the same time to do some useful work at the station. Other times, I enjoyed the luxury of bed and breakfast at Felixstowe. I found the train trip out from London a trifle nauseating, and being a keen cyclist preferred the journey over the fairly flat countryside, which I found far more enjoyable than the stuffy train ride.

Not that I am criticising the services offered in those days by the London and North Eastern Railway. In fact one enjoyable aspect was the excellent fruit lunch I could buy from the automatic vending machine which in those days stood at the foot of the stairs at Liverpool Street Station. I could then devour my meal en-route in luxurious, if sooty comfort.

Jack on his racing bicycle 1937. He probably used this bicycle to make the 140-mile round trip to Bawdsey each weekend. Perhaps he was on this bicycle when he joined the young German tourists.

In August 1938 I had spent a pleasant weekend by the sea, and on the Sunday I was cycling back to London. I gradually approached a long column of cyclists who were making a very fast pace. They were all dressed smartly in greenish shirts and, by English standards, very short khaki shorts. I tried to overtake them as we commenced climbing a long steep hill, but found the going hard. I spent the next few miles trailing the long column. The weather was very warm and with sweat dripping onto my low-dropped handlebars, I decided I could not beat the long column and would therefore have to join them. I drew up beside the last man in the formation who gave me a friendly smile before concentrating once again on breaking the back of the steep hill we were climbing. We travelled through a long dark forest over the hill and once on the downgrade I had a chance to look at the shirt he was wearing. It was covered in colourful badges and some words on his sleeves were obviously German. I tried to speak but my companions breathless English was poor and he indicated his inability to converse with a wide expanse of toothy smile.

Some distance further on the column leader signalled a halt and we wheeled off the road into a large tea garden. At my companions' invitation, I joined him for tea but only on condition that he would allow me to pay for the snack. With the help of one of his friends, we discussed cycling, life in Germany and life in the United Kingdom.

These sunburnt lads had been touring Kent and Sussex for almost two weeks; now they were near the end of their holiday and about to return to Germany. They told me how they enjoyed the beautiful English countryside, and would've liked to have stayed very much longer. It seems that most of them had already served a period of some form of military training and that the array of badges signified their progress in shooting, gliding, physical fitness and various other soldierly activities. They were a healthy happy-go-lucky crowd who enjoyed themselves immensely in the beautiful countryside. After a short break - much too short for me - they remounted, and were on their way. I scarcely had time to thank my new friend for his company before he waved goodbye leaving me to relax amidst the floral arches and lawns of this extremely attractive tea garden.

My rest completed, I once again got back on the road for the last stretch of my trip to London. The pleasant long summers evening gave me plenty of time to make big town before it grew dark and I made a steady pace. On reaching the top of a long, steep hill, I once again came across the German cyclists; bicycles discarded they lay by the side of the road on what I thought was a rather dangerously blind bend. The leader, together with one or two of the other men in the group, was hovering around a tripod-mounted camera. He seemed to be making a lot of fuss about a photograph, but I had noticed before that Germans were very fastidious about photography. From the top of this hill they had a panoramic view of the patchwork countryside stretching towards London. With the sun now beginning to set, the view was breathtaking.

It did not strike me at the time that the pictures they were taking might be used for something other than decorating a Teutonic family album. When some years later the Battle of Britain started, it became obvious that the

Luftwaffe had a very detailed knowledge of the English countryside. Perhaps some of these young cyclists with their broad smiles and eagles on their shirts had provided a portion of the material necessary for the preparation of Britain's 'Baptism by Fire'.

Chapter Two: Jack joins up

Jack on enlisting in 1940.

On the 29 February 1940 Jack (aged twenty) joined the RAF as a radio mechanic, and spent a month training at Uxbridge, with a spell at Morecombe where the esplanade was used by the RAF as a parade ground. With his pre-war knowledge of radar, he was posted in March to Yatesbury, in Wiltshire, training Radar personnel. He was very despondent about the outcome of the war.

He wrote:

It seemed as if the Luftwaffe could do as it pleased, burning and bombing where ever it chose. The stacked formations of bombers at times seem to swarm like locusts, and fill the sky. Worst of all we didn't seem to be able to do anything to resist the masses of squat black bombers.

On the face of it, there could be only one end to it all. We simply didn't stand a chance. If only they had listened to Churchill a few years ago, all this horror would never have happened. Now with all the petrol going up in smoke even a few fighters might be grounded.

I paid a visit to the balloon centre at Stanmore, not because I had the slightest interest in balloons; Stanmore was of course Lord Dowding's Fighter Command Headquarters. [Lord Dowding was responsible for the preparation and conduct of the Battle of Britain, from July to October 1940]. This was the one and only filter room, the receiving centre for all information on aircraft as plotted by the radar stations. Backed up by audible and visual reports issued by the Observer Corps, the presiding Command Controllers could immediately identify all aircraft plots as friendly or hostile. Security had been completely tightened up and after going for a short interview with a rather junior officer, I was told to go home and sit tight as I would soon be called up in the new special civilian organisation to be set up for RDF men.

Time went by, I carried on in my civilian radio work in the West End of London anxiously awaiting my call up, but maddeningly nothing transpired. My attempts to visit the radar stations with which I was acquainted, were now squashed and in desperation I went to Uxbridge RAF station, just to the west of London and made the most discreet enquiries about my future. Here I was immediately inducted into the new RAF branch. Eventually I heard we were to be called Radio Mechanics to distinguish us from the ordinary wireless electrical mechanics of the RAF.

Fortunately for all concerned the phoney war was on. Nothing was happening in France, and I sat on a barrack room bed at the RAF station in Uxbridge, with my head in my hands and waited impatiently. After my hectic life in London in the radio and television world, the enforced idleness was more than frustrating. Eventually after a short period of RAF disciplinary training at Uxbridge, I went off to Yatesbury in Wiltshire, Number One Radio School of the RAF. On our arrival at this, the original wireless school of the Royal Flying Corps., we found we were strange fowl amongst dozens of would-be wireless operators as nobody seemed to have any idea of what we were supposed to do.

Here I met one or two of the chaps with whom I had worked in the past and together we were detailed to assist in the building of the first radar school at a spot some distance from the main station, [identified as Hut 4]. Our time was spent in uncrating new secret equipment for the proposed establishment and it was while engaged in this task that I had an extremely depressing experience.

We were busily uncrating a top secret radar receiver known as RF6 manufactured by the Cossor wireless factory. This device was the acme of radar receivers at the time and incorporated every known device to secure superb results. It was an immensely secret machine, each and every one of its dozens of features likewise incredibly secret. It was a triumph of receiver design and demonstrated just how far forward the science had already progressed on the drawing board, as well as in the factory. This unit, which was brought down under special guard from the Cossor factory at Highbury in London, was carefully unpacked. We held our breath in awe as we gazed up at the 8 foot high monster. Carefully uncovering its shrouded face we were astounded to see scrawled across it's beautiful black face in white chalk, an enormous hammer and sickle. The political humorist who had, presumably, completed his artistic effort during the crating stage at the factory, did not even have the decency to avoid the delicate meter faces, the glasses of which had been pushed in and the internal movements sadly damaged. This deliberate vandalism by our own people was, to all of us, most depressing.

Though I would never have admitted it, I felt in my heart that we could not win this war. Russia and Germany had signed an alliance and here at home we were going to have to fight a Fascist and a Communist fifth column. It seemed as though we hadn't a hope. The fact that a mass of German bombers had not, as yet, arrived to destroy us, was, we understood, because Hitler could not believe that Britain did not once again intend to give in. Yet surely, they would come, and it appeared that besides contending with invading bombers we were also going to have to combat extreme political adherence on the home front.

Known British Fascists and Nazi sympathisers had been placed on the Isle of Man for the duration of the war, but who would know who the actual Nazi supporters were until they appeared as gauleiters after the German invasion and occupation of Great Britain. To me it was all very distressing and a further incident, which occurred at Yatesbury did nothing to alter my despondency.

At this time we received a short visit by three French Air Force officers. They were given official permission to be shown around and observe our radar activities. In their elegant dark blue uniforms they tiptoed around to avoid contaminating their shoes with the English mud, talking to nobody and, in general, gave all and sundry a pain in the neck.

In an effort to establish a local 'entente cordiale' with our allies I tried to converse with a man in my schoolboy French. When an urn of tea was sent out to us from the main camp, I tried to get beneath their aloofness and apparent disdain which at first, I had attributed to their inability to speak English. Diplomatically, and struggling with my strained vocabulary, I opened the conversation by criticising the quality of the NAAFI tea, the expressions of contempt on their faces doing little to assist my attempts at polite discourse. After a few words, I discovered they could speak excellent English, in fact a lot better than I could speak French, but as ever their handsome faces wore an almost perpetual sneer, the reason for which soon became apparent.

'You Tommies don't expect to beat the Boche with bits of wood and wire? Surely you know that they have thousands of armoured tanks and bombers. What good would all this be? Why indeed were we sent here to waste our time in this cold, windy and muddy place where it never stops raining?'

I pointed out that when the German army eventually attacked and had broken their heads on the Maginot line, they might try to flatten France with their bombers. Our job was to prepare, as quickly as possible, our own and Allied territories against air attack and this we were doing to the best of our ability. I told them that already some units had arrived in France; one under the famous technical writer and radio expert Flight Lieutenant Scott Taggart was already established there. [Later Wing Commander; he was responsible for Radar training at the Air Ministry].

The youngest of the Frenchmen told me that many French officers had already established a secret pact with their right wing organisation which still enjoyed a form of contact with the Nazis. This group, he said was well supported by the officer class of the three French fighting services. They could see no point in starting to fight and felt that negotiations with the Germans, before the main onslaught started, was far preferable to immediate defeat by the Luftwaffe and the German army.

I was staggered by the flagrant defeatism of these French airmen and realised the seriousness of their statements and the possible existence of a serious security breach. I brought the information, as it was expounded to me to the attention of one of the RAF officers on the site. He laughed it off as mere talk. He, being a rather keen radio ham, regarded the whole war as a wonderful game and an excellent chance to get to grips with the new and fantastic radio devices that he could never afford in peacetime. I did not insist that he took action, anyway he obviously thought the whole thing a joke.

Within a few months we were to learn to our cost, that many Frenchmen felt exactly the same way about the war and were in favour of a 'rapprochement' with the Nazis rather than risk the trial of strength. The military opportunists of the future will always have to be dealt with in the same way. There is no shortcut or easy way out. The twilight of freedom throughout the world will come when the major powers refuse to accept the challenge of the gauntlet thrown down by despotic military governments, seeking to force their will on their weaker neighbours.

Jack was part of a very select group at the beginning of the war. RDF, [Range and Direction Finding] as Radar was known, was a new science. Because of Jack's great interest in electronics and his work at Bawdsey with the inventor of Radar, Watson-Watt and his team, he was well-equipped to train others in the intricacies of this highly secret science. Very few people knew of its existence. Even pilots were unaware of how the 'radio engineers' were able to pinpoint enemy aircraft. There were very few skilled operators. His good friend John Strong was one. Together they were posted to North Foreland on the Kent coast. The Luftwaffe were mining the Thames Estuary. By plotting the German planes' flight paths, the RDF operators were able to advise the minesweepers of the 'rough' line of mines that were laid each time which saved much searching the waters.

Jack continues:

'Never volunteer for anything!' warned our moaning Willy.

'How do you feel about it John?'

'I'm game,' he replied.

We both shot our right arms into the air.

'Stick your neck out and you'll get it chopped off.' Willy counselled.

'Look!' said John Strong, 'Things generally are in a hell of a mess, we must do anything we can to help. I don't know about you but that is why I joined.'

We were at an RAF signals camp just after Dunkirk [26 May – 4 June 1940]. Under secret cover, a request had been made for some temporarily, technical RDF [later known as Radar] known assistance, exact duties not specified. There were still a minute number of people with radar training, and in our opinion it was an honour to be able to join in the air battle which was obviously getting underway. The Luftwaffe was now making probing attacks around most of the English coast line.

Collecting our small kit and enough clothing for about a week, we climbed aboard an RAF truck and headed for Swindon where we entrained and travelled east to London. There were six in our party, and we had plenty of time during the journey to discuss what fate might possibly have in store for us. The phoney war had ended and the German army had passed through France like a knife through butter. It was good to know that we would be doing something really constructive towards the war effort. We were routed through Bromley, a London suburb, where 60 Group had its local wing headquarters. Here we were broken into pairs, John and I climbed onto the back of a small Bedford truck, which immediately got on the road which I knew quite well. We made towards Maidstone and Canterbury, a road on which in happier days I had travelled many times on my racing cycle. As we approached the narrow, winding streets of Canterbury, the air was heavily pockmarked with the bursts from ack-ack shells as the German aircraft were now beginning to appear in quite large numbers over the Kent countryside. We stopped for a short time in a narrow lane and watched the intense activity overhead. Though there were very few fighters they were giving a very good account of themselves. The jarring rattle of the guns and the horror and death stalking the clouds over our heads was completely out of keeping with the beautiful green countryside. Eventually we carried on and made our way down to the coast at Broadstairs, a pleasant seaside resort on the North Foreland.

There was plenty of air activity and we accepted this without any particular interest and made no attempt to define details of any particular operations. We had become quite blasé to the whole business. From Broadstairs we were routed to the northernmost tip of the North Foreland. We dropped off the back of our truck at the entrance to one of the new CHL [Chain Home Low stations which could see at a lower altitude as opposed to the original Chain Home] stations that were already coming into service and acting as low cover for the CH stations that could not see aircraft much below 3000ft [915m].

After our identity cards had been carefully checked at the makeshift orderly room we were placed on duty, immediately. We had no idea exactly what to do, but common sense readily made up for our lack of knowledge. This was one of the ramshackle almost homemade stations that Dr John Cockroft himself had recently commissioned. [Sir John Cockroft was a brilliant physicist who was later appointed Head of the Air Defence Research and Development Establishment. He later won the Nobel Prize for his research into nuclear fission] He had already done great work in combatting the magnetic mines at the approaches to the Port of London.

From Foreness, looking north-east one could scan the Dutch and German skies. Due west, we could look along the Kent coast towards London and the Thames Estuary. Looking to east we enjoyed a long range snoop of German air operations in their newly acquired French aerodromes. Although the Germans usually carried out their air movements in complete radio silence in an effort to avoid the British developing an intelligence picture, they did not realise that we were plotting their build-up of formations in French territory long before they set course for England.

Though, in size, the 20ft [6m] high CHL station masts were dwarfed by the 360ft [109m] masts of a CH station, the smaller unit was a giant in technical performance. We were to assist and do anything that was required; to act as operators or, if the equipment broke down, to assist in its repair and to be on standby in case of breakdowns. On the short strip of the Kentish Foreland coast there were two other giant radars which were already doing Trojan work. The first was Dover CH and further west, CH Dungeness. Although we could not plot at the speed of a CH station, we had a far greater accuracy and a plotting was not marred by the serious ambiguities that often accompanied mini CH plots of enemy aircraft and formations. The CHL however could not read the height of an aircraft or formation as could the huge CH station.

At that time there was a great scarcity of technical men available for the operation of this radically new type of radar equipment and the station was shockingly short staffed. Due to the highly specialised nature and secrecy of the work, nobody could be brought in from the outside to assist and long hours were the order of the day and night. Like all other radar units, the station was operational 24 hours a day which included a supposed hour a day off the air for maintenance. During this hour the local CH station, Dover, was always warned that we would no longer be giving low cover and to be doubly alert.

In the small operations room of the CHL, one rotated the hand pedals which turned the roof aerials [40ft wide x 20ft tall], with your eyes glued to the green flickering 3241 tube [cathode ray tube] and waited for the appearance of an aircraft blip. The drill was quite simple. The range of the aircraft was read off the screen and the bearing was a read off a crude, but accurate scale mounted on the aerial drive column. The resultant plot of range and bearing was marked with a pencil on the tracing paper clamped over a military grid map and the four figure coordinate pinpoint read over the telephone to Fighter Command Headquarters, Stanmore.

It was a most exciting station as German aircraft cruising over France could be seen at almost any time of the day or night. German aircraft flying at ten to fifteen thousand feet could be clearly seen up to seventy miles inside France where the Luftwaffe was now taking up residence.

After a thrilling spell in the operations room, seeing and plotting aircraft, one had to take a turn in the transmitter hut; once again this entailed turning by hand the pedals that rotated the massive transmitter aerial, but this time blindly following the receiver aerial by the simple expedient of keeping the needle of a small electrical meter continuously on zero. In the early hours of the morning this could be an extreme form of torture.

Sitting in the small hut with the transmitter towering over you and droning its way through the night, was in itself no hardship. Though these early transmitters used the enormously high voltage of twenty-five thousand volts, that was in itself not in any way dangerous as the thick sheet steel sides and excellent manufacturing technique, made the transmitter perfectly safe from X- radiation.

The T3056 [transmitter] had one rather hair-raising, if not dangerous, idiosyncrasy. At times, usually during the early hours of the morning when the air became damp, the high-voltage system broke down the air insulation and a fantastic scream ensued from the iron walls of the transmitter. This screaming 25,000 V cacophony vibrated the heavy steel walls of the transmitter as if they were made of rice paper. This ear-splitting racket occurred with no warning and everybody in the early hours when you were battling to keep your eyes open and the needle on the zero. [This phenomenon is called a corona].

Outside the transmitter hut everything would be peaceful and quiet. With the Luftwaffe across the channel in France all nicely tucked in, we, however, were on a twenty four hour watch and dare not relax even during the quiet and peaceful predawn hours. This screaming corona would suddenly burst upon you, all but throwing you out of your chair in fright. As you left the pedals to stop the racket, the telephone would invariably scream hysterically at you and the operator would demand that you get the aerials back in line. On hearing the corona racket over the telephone he would understand, and sympathetically hang up.

The standard treatment was to wind the transmitter high-voltage system down to three thousand volts and then once the corona had stopped, to gradually increase the voltage back to its normal twenty-five thousand volts. Needless to say the acoustic shock left one with palpitations for some ten minutes afterwards.

During the daylight hours there was now intense air activity, friendly and hostile, though there seemed to be no great danger to CHL Foreness. Having been allocated a BSA motorcycle in case urgent spares were required, we often made trips to the CH station at Dover and even further afield.

We struck up a friendship with the daily changing occupants, pilots and ground crew of the fighter aerodrome dispersal tent, about two miles inland. Sometimes we kicked a ball around with these lads and we always brought and exchanged rations of chocolates and sweets.

Their two or three Hurricanes could not be seen from the sea as they were located snugly behind a mound which acted as anti-blast hill, masking their presence. Camouflage netting, plus the natural camouflage painted on the hurricanes, made them extremely difficult to spot from the air.

After a short and hectic game of football one afternoon, John and I lay on the soft grass panting and the pilots returned to the bell tent for a rest. All was quiet and peaceful. We vaguely heard the muted note of some aircraft engines which John, with his excellent eyesight located while they were out to sea and coming in our direction. Low-flying aircraft from the three aerodromes in our vicinity, Hawkinge, Lympne and Manston were always around so the appearance of two aircraft cruising low over the sea seemed to be just another patrolling section of fighter aircraft.

As there had been no fighter scramble, we paid little attention to them as they grew larger, in no time they were almost overhead. In the blinding sunlight we stood up to greet them as they cruised low, directly over our heads when with a shock we saw the huge black crosses of Messerschmitt 109. The pilots must have seen us, but decided that they had more important things to do with their ammunition rather than strafing a pair of stupid civilians. We were thankful for the fact that they flew right over the blast hill and camouflage fighters, without seeing a thing and sailed serenely inland.

Running to the dispersal tent I frantically wound the field telephone and reported the two enemy aircraft which nobody had seen or reported. Flying very low they had avoided intentionally or otherwise, pick up by our radar.

It was apparent at times that the Luftwaffe now regarded this forward area of Kent as part of their own happy hunting grounds and did just as they liked.

Eventually a signal arrived requesting us to come back to London for another posting. We were informed, unofficially by the orderly room, that there was a possibility, at the Manston aerodrome, of a lift to London the next day with some returning war correspondents. They had a large car for just the two of them. We made our way to the aerodrome and after a considerable wait managed to contact the English war correspondent. We pointed out that we were specialist technicians and it was not exactly the right time to be kicking our heels on the Kent railway station, when we had other most urgent but undefined duties to perform. This gentleman showed his teeth apologetically, and seemed rather unenthusiastic. John Strong immediately tackled the Yank who had just appeared on the scene. This burly fellow nearly bent over backwards in extending an invitation to both of us to accompany them on the trip back to London.

We climbed aboard, amid one of the now almost continuous air raid alerts. With our little blue bags and our neatly folded overcoats, we vanished into the rear seat of the roomy Humber Snipe with 11 fighter group markings. Our American friend took up most of the middle seat with his bulky frame. Beside him carefully on his seat, he placed his large travelling bag which emitted gaily clinking noises every time it was moved. The English correspondent sat beside the RAF driver in the front. The American expressed a desire for a coastal trip. As the driver was not familiar with Kent, I directed him towards Margate and made towards Whitstable. We climbed the steep hill to join the east coast and caught a glimpse of the CH Whitstable. "That's a hell of a dangerous place to put a radio station" said the Yank. John looked at me meaningfully, but we did not say a word. The secret nature of the station's operations disallowed us from even venturing a remark. In fact it was perfectly placed for its major part in the Battle of Britain, which had just started. The other correspondent tartly pointed out that we had not expected France to collapse quite so easily and make this the front line.

"Yes," the Yank agreed sagely, "If the Froggies had barricaded the streets of Paris they could've held the German army at bay for years."

This I am sure was the chip that General De Gaulle had carried on his shoulder to this very day. Gay Paris was declared an open city and the German soldiers could not conceal their delight at the ease with which they had rectified their defeat in the First World War. To London and not Paris went the honour of putting a halt to the Nazi invaders. When in fact London was preparing for the Blitz, Paris was already experiencing a business boom when the

German troops began to off load their occupation money.

As we travelled onwards towards London our American friend did most of the talking. John, never at all talkative, listened; I put in a few ayes and nays, but the English correspondent said just nothing. The Yank delved into his roomy bag and brought forth a bottle of French brandy which he uncorked and handed to the driver. The English correspondent recoiled in horror, when the driver took a swig straight from the bottle. Both John and I were not great drinkers, but we went through the motions of taking a snort. A little while later, just before I fell asleep I noted that the English newspaper man was simply horrified when the driver took a long steady drink as we were tearing down the Rose Hill to Chatham. Travelling at great speed, he wiped his mouth and narrowly missed the buttress supporting the bridge at the foot of the hill.

The next thing I knew was when we were entering south east London and the RAF driver was discussing with the correspondents, the column of black smoke and vapour trails that hung in the sky ahead. This was not exactly surprising as the enemy bombers had been hard at work all day. Using the Blackwall tunnel, we passed under the Thames and made our way towards London Bridge and the City.

It was early evening when we stopped near the Daily Telegraph building in Fleet Street. Its familiar shiny face, which I knew so well, seemed so homely and friendly after the strange life we had been leading.

We piled out of our transport and the English correspondent took his leave. At the invitation of the Yank, we accompanied him to a public house behind the Telegraph building, just off Fleet Street and we sat down to an excellent meal of good old English roast beef, Yorkshire pudding and two veg. Whilst we hungry airmen, who had not had a decent meal in weeks, got cracking on the food, our American host spent most of his time between the table, the telephone and the bar. He was a wonderful and dynamic personality enjoying every moment of his hectic life. After he'd got his food which I don't think he particularly enjoyed, despite our protests, he paid for his food as well as our own and left the pub in a great hurry.

There was far too much doing for this man to sit still.

This was my initial introduction to Quentin Reynolds, the famous war correspondent. Years after the war, we were both unknowingly to feature in the biggest libel trial in US history[5].

A short year later my friend, John Strong was [missing presumed] killed in action defending a mobile radar station against a German paratroop assault, during the invasion of Greece.

---

[5] The story of the Quentin Reynold's libel trial is featured in chapter 16.

Following his induction and training at Uxbridge and Yatesbury, Jack was sent to the far north of Scotland, Rosehearty north of Aberdeen. The Germans could easily attack the British fleet from their bases in Norway. Rosehearty was near the port of Fraserburgh; Kinnaird Head was the headland that sheltered the small fishing port. It being the closest part of the British mainland to Norway was important for tracking the arrival of German bombers coming from Norway to attack Scottish ports and factories.

Z. 183   Rosehearty from the North.

This postcard was bought by Jack; it shows a view of Rosehearty taken from the sea.

From Rosehearty Jack started writing to his girlfriend, Dally, who would later become his wife and my mother. His letters were everything that one could expect from a young lovestruck airman working in intensely secret work, in a harsh location, far from home, and never knowing when, and if, he would see the love of his life again.

Dally, Jack's sweetheart in 1941

The great responsibility on his shoulders, (he was barely 20), took its toll. He was deprived of sleep and always cold. He seemed to be ill frequently, with coughs and colds, depressed by lack of sleep and worry that Germany had the upper hand. His constant worry about the family was evident in his writings and personal letters.

To add to that, he was grieving for his maternal

grandfather, who died on 19 October 1939, his father, and also his maternal grandmother in the same year. The war had just started, and Jack's mother Annie had lost both her parents and her husband within a year. She had had a late baby, Harold born 12 February 1939. For a young twenty-year-old, Jack knew that even without the war, his mother's circumstances were dire.

The CHL Radar station where Jack was posted comprised of a couple of unheated huts on a windy cliff top in the far north of Scotland. These housed the RDF (Radar) equipment and a hut with the generator, inside a compound surrounded by barbed wire fences. At the gated entrance was another hut occupied by the Gordon Highlanders army personnel charged with providing security.

Jack was billeted with the Buchan family at 37 Pitsligo Street and seemed to spend quite a bit of time avoiding the advances of the girls of the village.

Pitsligo St., Rosehearty.

Jack was billeted with Mr & Mrs Buchan at 37 Pitsligo Street, Rosehearty. Another postcard bought by Jack while he was posted there.

18 August 1940

Some people have been evacuated but none of the girls seem to have gone. We had a dance the other night during which a Jerry kite [German bomber] came over the village. The lights were put out and I had a girl round my neck trying to convince me that she was windy [scared]. Since I didn't fancy her or any other girl, I experienced a "relief of Mafeking" thrill when the van came to pick us up.

15 June 1941

Possibly you don't know it but they, i.e. the girls are constantly devising means of annoying me. Latest is my general attitude towards Scots girls. I was invited to a party a short time ago. Knowing the characters and habits of the ladies!!! organising the party, I decided that I was too busy to go.

Unfortunately one came to our house on eve of the party and found me at home.

After finding it impossible to get me out, she began referring to me as an English snob, refusing to associate with the beggarly Scots girls.

I'm afraid that I got rather annoyed and said things she entirely misinterpreted and next thing I knew she was crying. I changed my line and partially consented to go to the party and she stopped crying immediately.

The change was so abrupt that I decided it must have been crocodile tears and told her to go for a run. The air went absolutely black and blue with Scotch swear words that would burn up this paper.

Well I didn't go and I'm glad I didn't. The various happenings were the scandal of Rosehearty next morn.

I won't go into details, in fact I don't know why I've wasted this much paper; but it showed me the machinations of nefarious females.

I will now skip the scandal and speak of something worth talking about. Possibly you realise that as soon as a bloke has had leave, his most urgent problem on return to his unit is securing further leave, and considering how and where he will spend it.

27 June 1941

The morals are extremely low and I prefer to remain aloof, and interested in radio.
I would rather be with a 50,000 volt generator, than any girl.

He travelled frequently, training new recruits, often on secret orders. He was not permitted to say where he travelled, so unfortunately his war service record is not that detailed. Our family legend has it that at one point my mother was writing to him in Scotland, when actually he was 'round the corner' in London working secretly.

Dally's younger brother Frank now lives with his wife Irma in Los Angeles. We chat often and occasionally he remembers another memory of his wartime childhood.

In February 2022, he came up with a gem. Did I know, he asked, that when my mother was writing love letters to Jack at his radar station in the frozen north of Scotland, part of the time Jack was secretly working "around the corner" in the Yardley Perfume Factory? The Yardley factory was a short distance from where Dally was living. Irma said she was a young girl when she became friendly with Frank, but also remembered the family talking about the fact that Jack was "so near, and yet so far!"

I was understandably bowled over by this revelation.

Jack's letters are full of longing for his next meeting with Dell but also the urgent need for absolute secrecy about his whereabouts. How difficult it must have been (if this was indeed true) to have been minutes away and not have attempted to see her, or revealed where he was working.

In this book I have attempted to confirm every fact I have written. Would I be able to verify Frank's story? Basil and I immediately contacted whoever we could think of who may confirm Frank's revelation.

There was now a deadline for the book. Time was short, Basil's initial efforts came to nought.

He wrote to Yardley; they did not respond.

We asked several people if they knew what went on at the factory. Rachael Abbiss, senior curator at the Battle of Britain Bunker Museum suggested writing to the local archives (Newham) to see if they had any information. Jess Conway, the archivist wrote back almost instantly to say she would ask around. A few days later she sent us some leads including a book that has been written about the factory during the war. Kate Thompson's "Secrets of the Lavender Girls".

In it a Yardley supervisor states that two of the floors in the factory were devoted to making, amongst other things "anti-radar devices". So, there it was. Frank's memory was very accurate.

Jack writes in *The Wizard War:*

At the clifftop we worked in a little station, but the village people I knew who we were billeted with were allowed to know nothing of our secret defence work. Our RAF insignias gave them cause to expect some sort of protection from us, protection that we could in no way directly supply.

A sharp attack was carried out on the harbour of Fraserburgh. Bombs were dropped and for the small fishing town the casualties were very high. Ships of a convoy rounding the headland near the town were attacked and a few were sunk. These bombers had been plotted by our radar system for almost an hour before they attacked the town and the ships. After passing the plots on any responses seen on our radar tubes to Stanmore, our responsibility ended, and we were powerless and unable to do anything more. The long delays caused by the information on the aircraft position having to go first to London, caused two Hurricanes to appear from Dyce [now Aberdeen airport] long after the action was finished. As the days went by, the masts of many sunken ships came to be part of the coastal scenery and were planted permanently amongst the rocks of this rugged headland.

Surviving building at the site of the radar station at Rosehearty

In desperation, I personally submitted certain proposals to assist in the interception of the bombers, based upon the basic navigational knowledge I had accumulated from my RAF friends before the war. This was sent to 60 Group, our headquarters near London, under secret cover. Without knowing it I had proposed the GCI (Ground Control Interception) system more or less as it had already been set up and prepared by the boffins in the south. I received no concrete answers to the various suggestions I put forward through the official channels to Leighton Buzzard. In fact it was suggested by another member of the station that I forget about improving navigational systems and worry more about technical improvements to the station. In my opinion the performance of the CHL was more than satisfactory, the problem was insufficient use was being made of the information we were supplying.

I decided to somehow or other put one or two of my ideas on aircraft interception into practice, illegally! As the lives and security of the Scots people were involved I enlisted assistance from a Scots mechanic who claimed vehemently that he was a Scottish Nationalist. His name was William McKenzie. I appealed to him to assist me in my machinations. The plan was quite simple. The scheme was based upon the fact that on the shortwave radio, a TR1082/1083 combination held on the station, the German pilots could be clearly heard in their flying formations as they had left Norway and long before we actually picked them up on our radar screen.

Once on the radar screens we watched them for at least half an hour before they reached our area. We would then observe their leisurely low sweep over the sea, machine-gunning fishing boats and doing just as they liked. They could fly with impunity anywhere. Sometimes they went north towards the Orkney Islands and sometimes south to Aberdeen. Our headland pointed like a beckoning finger to their base. This point became the Luftwaffe's most successful hunting ground. On the radio with their 'Victor ein zwei drei" the gutteral voices of the German pilots receiving their navigational leaders' course changes simply blasted through on my radio.

I decided to try and confuse the German airmen by playing tricks with their navigational system. By receiving the signal from their powerful beacon near Stavanger and feeding it into my little transmitter I feel I made life a bit difficult for the enemy navigator. On one occasion I received the satisfaction of hearing a block of unmistakable German invective from one of the aircraft but I'm not sure at whom it was directed! I also attempted to jam this homing wave length once they were on their way back to Norway, but I very much doubt whether anything worthwhile was achieved. It was at least a positive action and better than biting one's fingernails.

To keep my scheme going, the major problem was to arrange for the charging of the car battery, which powered the transmitter. This became quite flat even after a short periods of operation and early the following morning I had the task of staggering down to the village with this heavy battery on my back for a recharge. If nothing else this helped to develop my back muscles.

Surviving building, Rosehearty and the sea beyond.

My father was always handy with car problems. Once they were travelling in Kruger National Park and the car had exhaust problems. He asked all his passengers to chew gum and made a temporary stop for the exhaust out of a ball of gum.

This was quite fortunate, as wild animals would not appreciate a very noisy moving vehicle in their territory!

Chapter Three: Scottish Winter

My parents used to joke about the bus driver at the Speen bus stop. Speen is a tiny hamlet near High Wycombe where Dally was evacuated with her work. She spent much of her spare time in Speen with her cousins Ann and Dell and their families. Ivor, Dell's son, still remembers Jack's visits. Ivor's family were billeted in a small house after spending weeks in an old gypsy caravan, with a bed for nine! When my mother came to stay, she slept in the caravan. We have a picture of her standing outside, with a good friend she made, Hilda, who lived in Speen. Visits from Jack were rare.

The family joke was, that if my father hadn't been chivvied on by the bus conductor to kiss my mother goodbye as he left, he might never have asked her to marry him. Whenever they teased one another about their marriage, they would say "If it wasn't for that bus driver...!"

The following letter describes how Jack, writing from Scotland had to screw up an enormous amount of courage for that first kiss!

37 Pitsligo St.,
Rosehearty
Aberdeenshire

21 May 1941

My Dear Dally,

I have little news of an interest to communicate so I have propped up your photograph to give me some inspiration.

All the chaps on my crew know you very well; by sight anyway, because your photograph is always in a strategic position when I'm at work. Everybody without scarcely any exceptions, thinks that it is a film star picture.

There is Bill Ramage one of my pals who thinks his girl is tops. And another lad Gordon Colman who thinks his is the most beautiful. Well we often compare pictures, and yours leaves them all standing.

All the happy (single) chaps here want to know how to contact you. The things they say would make you blush. Still I won't repeat them.

In your last letter you took me to task for suggesting that you might kiss any old thing. Well of course I didn't mean it.

I feel exactly the same way about the same subject. I never kissed anybody after I reached the age of fifteen. It seemed to me as distasteful as somebody using my toothbrush. If somebody were to borrow it just once I would never use it again. I'd much rather buy a new one.

For a helluva time back I've been like that about letting somebody borrow my lips. The amazing part is that though I have always dodged slobbering over loving aunts etc, and kept clear of those games which necessitated slobbering, I always wanted to sample just one pair and one pair only.

Appreciating the fact that I have a face like the

back of a bus, none of the so called personality and sex appeal I had given it up.

Though I had practically given up every hope of even sampling the unobtainable goods, I used to think and dream about it continuously. Sometimes I nearly went frantic but couldn't do anything about it.

Well I joined up when this rotten war began and I got worse than ever. When I chanced to see the possession of the forbidden fruits my knees used to buckle under me, and I think I acted like a wet sack.

Before I came back on leave I would kind of prepare a plan of campaign that would always go haywire. The last time I came on leave I had made up my mind to have a darned good try. As usual I obviously didn't stand a chance and after about twelve of my fourteen days leave had gone, I was feeling dejected and really ill.

I began to develop my old tummy ache, and prepared to go back to Hearty Rose. That particular morning my mother was moaning and grumbling at me. I was feeling rotten and she made me worse.

I decided that if nothing else, I was at least going to try to see the owner of the aforementioned pair of luscious lips.

So armed with a ridiculous excuse, I proceeded forthwith to the village in which dwelt luscious lips and owner.

In a way I suppose the excuse was a worthy one.

My intention was to get a place out of the blitz for my sister to live in. As you know this ended in a fiasco but it wasn't our fault.

Joy of joys came when both lips and owner accompanied me on search of village for digs for beautiful sister.

Finished tour of village with my companion almost walking on her knees, she was so tired. But like a hero she stuck to her post until duty was done.

Proceeded to cousins of beautiful lady who had been walking on knees and waited. After considerable waiting, lips and owner walked through the door; was I pleased.

Spent as much time as possible looking at lady and lips and then escorted her to bus. Bus was not ready to go. Waited with me almost completely buckled and heart with tonsils.

Driver of bus drops some advice re Aspros [he probably suggested some aspirin to fortify him] and takes position at front of bus. Zero hour.

My immediate thought was "I won't see her for months now, should I risk it."

As you know, I did. I don't know who was shocked most, you or I.

It was amazing how drunk I felt. Actually I can't remember anything after, until I reached the garden gate. You'd better remember the intoxicating power of your kisses or somebody will be getting into trouble.

You will no doubt think me a chump for telling you all this but I'll stop now in case you don't like it. Silly as it may sound I feel a lot better writing all this tripe down, it has relieved me considerably.

If only for that reason I hope you don't mind. I'll try to write a more interesting letter next time.

Please excuse the horrible writing but I've been trying to put it down quickly. I'll sign off now, and once again I faithfully promise you a less selfish letter next time,

yours,

Jack.

Hilda, who owned the caravan, with Dell in Speen, near High Wycombe in 1941. Dell stayed in the caravan as did her cousin Anne, Anne's husband and two sons. According to Ivor Glazer, he his brother and their parents also occupied the caravan as the house they had been evacuated to was not ready. So nine of them slept in the caravan from time to time. It was at the bus stop in Speen that Jack gave Dell her first kiss. The firm Dell worked for was moved to West Wycombe to escape the bombing.

Jack certainly needed thoughts of Dally to keep him warm. On occasion, he would have been justified in thinking the weather was his enemy, rather than the German bombers.

He writes in *The Wizard War* manuscript....

It seemed that the coming of Spring in March 1941 was in itself no safeguard against the snow in this windy north east corner of Scotland.

It was already snowing when we went on duty for the evening watch and we sat shivering in the unheated room of the CHL station, which needed all the electric power that could be supplied by the 15 kVA diesel electric system. There was no reserve power for electric heaters and at that time no paraffin stoves were available to us.

Housed in the same compound as the CHL station were the men of the Gordon Highlanders who were on guard duty. They paraded around the perimeter, stamping their feet and blowing the snow from their moustaches. They greeted us with the typical Aberdonian "Fine day", which was the stock in trade greeting, even if it was raining cats and dogs. As the snow fell from the grey skies it grew dark and a vicious north-east wind blew up. The wind abated somewhat and then the snow began to come down in earnest.

It snowed throughout the night and by morning the ground was covered in a mantle of beautiful clean white snow. After that night watch, we donned our greatcoats and trudged our way down to our billets in the village of Rosehearty. Feeling tired after the long night's duty we staggered and plunged our way down the hill. After a hearty breakfast of bros [Scottish porridge] and sausage cooked by Mrs Buchan, by nine o'clock I was fast asleep. It snowed steadily throughout the day, the thick flakes dropping vertically down. Due to the abject shortage of staff we were to go on duty again that night. With my host, Mr John Buchan, I inspected the air raid shelter which we had tried to cut out of the rocks. It was obliterated now by the heavy fall of snow. After tea I pulled on my two pairs of ski stockings and fitted my gumboots over the top of them. With two jerseys under my RAF tunic followed by my great-coat, service gas mask and sou'wester, I collected my friends of the watch, and we ploughed our way slowly up the hill to the radar station.

The wind had been rising, and the snow was now at times assuming a horizontal trajectory as we staggered into the operations room. We arrived in the middle of an animated scene. The hand-rotated bicycle chain that turned the windmill-like aerial at some 20 feet above our heads, had snapped in the gale. Two members of the duty crew were on the roof of the hut holding the massive aerial [the aerials were 40 foot across and 20 foot high] whilst an Air Ministry technician, Archie Blair, effected the repairs. With a flourish the I/C watch signed off in the logbook, and we took up our stations for the evening. One man went to the transmitter hut to bind the transmitter aerial and the other three members of the crew settled down in the operations room which was about fifty yards away. Snow or no snow, the CHL had to keep on the air and survey the skies above the massive shipping convoys coming round the top of Scotland at Thurso and our headland at

Fraserburgh and Peterhead.

Already the heavy snow had claimed some victims. One local man who had missed the road up from Macduff, a small township a few miles from Rosehearty, had been found by a policeman; the local had died of exposure. Life for these hardy folk was indeed a trial during the winter months.

Stanmore informed me that there was a very little doing. This telephone link with civilisation made life bearable. It was strange to be exchanging chatter with people a short bus ride from my home in London, whilst we sat marooned seven [sic] hundred miles to the north, watching for enemy raiders.

It was definitely impossible weather for aircraft, but information on convoy movements on the heavily mined route was always needed by the Naval Liaison Officer at Aberdeen Naval Base, seventy miles to our south.

Though the room was cold, with a blanket or two we achieved a measure of protection from the icy blast outside. Careful doctoring of the blackout shutters with blankets made the room comparatively snug, but certainly not warm. There were, of course, no beds, so the airmen not actually watching the screen or operating the transmitter were usually to be found stretched out on the floor behind the receiver where the warm air from the power plant circulated. The hard concrete floor was not exactly the most luxurious of beds and one always woke for a turn at the tube with a sigh of relief, and usually a stiff neck, from an errant draught.

This method of rest was highly conducive to nightmares. One night one of our AM [Air Ministry] technicians, a short, plump, young Yorkshire man, Bill Iredale, let out a terrific yell in his sleep. In a panic I tore round to the back of the receiver to see if he had accidentally electrocuted himself by touching the 6000 V power supply for the cathode ray tubes. In fact he was kneeling away from me with his head down on the ground and his bottom up in the air. With his fingers he held onto a small duct on the floor which enclosed the power cables. He was fast asleep in this queer posture and also in the middle of a nightmare. As I arrived he yelled out at the top of his voice in his broad nasal accent "I'm oopsahd down! ee I'm oopsahd down." Apparently he thought he was falling off a cliff and his moment had come.

Outside, the gale was piling the snow up in enormous drifts and the buffeting wind made it impossible to turn the aerials smoothly. Our struggle with the binding pedals was terminated by the telephone ringing from the transmitter hut. The worst had happened, his chain had snapped and had snaked upwards to be ground into the gear wheels. It was irreparable, and the forty foot aerial was now in danger of being smashed by the gale force wind that was hammering the aerial system backwards and forwards. I put on my greatcoat and sou'wester and told an operator to report the station off the air. I went out in the wind and snow and over to the transmitter hut with some thick rope to lash the aerial in an easterly direction.

I climbed the twenty-foot ladder and hung onto the wooden frame at the base of the aerial system. I crawled around the turntable to the other side of the gantry while another operator came up to steady the aerial from the ladder side. Whilst I was preparing the lashing, a vicious gust of wind caught the aerial and knocked my companion from his perch on the ladder onto the ground. Another operator took his place and I lashed the aerial facing the usual direction from which hostile aircraft came, the east. Luckily my fallen friend had landed on the roof of the hut in the soft snow, unhurt.

Looking over towards the barrack hut that housed our Gordons [Highlanders], which I could now only vaguely see, I was surprised to note that it had almost completely disappeared under a snowdrift. On our windward side, the snow had already reached the top of the blast walls of both huts. We started back to the operations room, leaning almost horizontally into the wind and snow and took off our sou'westers which now stood up by themselves on the floor. They were stiff with ice.

This was not the end to our troubles as we then found that the line to Stanmore was no longer working. I decided that to avoid damage to our now useless receiver aerial, we had better lash it on the same bearing as the transmitter aerial. It was intensely cold. The Gordon guards had given us some food. Fortified by some bully beef and biscuits and some black watery cocoa, my lads laid down together to try and get warm with the aid of a blanket or two. I sat down in front of the radar tube and watched, with the telephone head set in position just in case Stanmore came back on the line.

Slowly the night went by, but by eight o'clock next morning the blizzard had not abated and I began to worry about our diesel fuel position. Putting on our greatcoats and sou'westers we fought our way to the transmitter hut besides which the diesel was located. Even the transmitter hut was now difficult to find. We had to dig our way down through the snow to refuel the diesel, which had chugged steadily and comfortably on. If it had stopped and cooled down, we would never have been able to start it again.

I checked that the man in the transmitter hut was comfortable and as I opened the door, I was greeted by a nice satisfying smell of fried kipper. We were too late, however, as our crafty friend had already disposed of the delicacy. Apparently he had cooked a kipper by switching off the transmitter, fixing into lock on a 25,000 V-V1901 rectifier valve and hanging the kipper around its neck. This valve operated at an enormously high temperature and cooked a kipper to a turn!

Paddy [the transmitter operator] was happy, so we left him to it. This time we struggled madly to find our own operations room. It was almost impossible to breathe in the blizzard, even behind our greatcoat lapels. By now it was long past breakfast time and we were all hungry, but there was no way of even getting to the Gordons, despite their close proximity. With telephones out of action, we were cut off from the world. We stood our sou'westers where the water would drain away [in the Radar hut] and decided to wait until the blizzard subsided somewhat.

Evening came and we were still waiting, and to make matters worse one of the older members of our crew was having stomach cramps, mainly I suppose from the cold and lack of food. Food has never really worried me greatly and I was feeling fine despite the cold. After a particularly bad spasm from my elderly friend, I decided to try and reach the Gordons' site in an effort to obtain cocoa, at least. This time I had to fight to open the door and was appalled at the ferocity of the cold blast. Outside it was quite impossible to breathe and I struggled to shut the door as quickly as possible. I was however determined to give it a try and in my full regalia but this time with two sou'westers, I started off with a gas mask in position to allow me to breathe and a long five-cell torch for light. It should still have been light but the blizzard wiped out any vestige of daylight. I stood for a moment outside the blast wall of the hut and decided in which direction the Gordons' hut must lie. I started walking, my gumboots sinking deeply into the snow and walked as well as I could with the snow constantly filling the glasses on my gas mask. Switching on the powerful torch, for a moment I thought it was not working, putting its glass flush with the glass of my gas mask, I perceived a faint glimmer; turning round, I noted with dismay that the holes made by my gumboots were rapidly filling with snow.

This was my only means of finding my way back to the operations room. I decided to go back immediately, and I retraced my steps with the holes getting fainter and fainter, I panicked and plodded and half fell back into the remains of my footsteps until they were all blotted out. I carried on intending to persevere in the same direction and crashed face - first into the blast wall, which I could not see. Feeling my way around, I eventually found the opening and then went through the door, stumbling into the middle of the room where I leaned on the receiver for support, trying to regain sufficient strength to remove my various wrappings.

Some time later I tried to make the fifty-yard trip, but with the same results. It was a hazardous undertaking, for had I been unable to find my way back to our hut, I would have suffered the same fate as the man from MacDuff. It was impossible to see, and difficult to breathe out there in the blizzard and without shelter, nobody could have survived.

In an effort to raise both the morale and the temperatures of the men I started a sing-song and got the lads to tell jokes. Their enthusiasm, however, had already flagged at the prospect of spending another night in the hut with the blizzard howling outside. This appealed to no one. Taking the four-foot sheet-iron side covers off the radar receiver, I made the invalid sit between them so that his body temperature might be maintained somewhat higher by the hot air emanating from the hundred or more valves in the receiver.

An uncomfortable night passed. When I judged it must be daylight, I went to the door. I noted that the steady gale had dropped and was pleased to see that the snow was not falling almost vertically. Only now and again did a gust stir the peaceful snow and remind us how violent had been the blizzard of the night before. The sky seemed to have got a fraction lighter. Putting on my greatcoat and sou'wester, I once again attempted to locate the Gordons. Before I departed, my invalid friend pleaded with me to try and get some water. We had tried warming snow, but it simply made him retch.

Through the steadily falling snow I walked in the correct direction, but when I reasoned that I had long passed the hut I still could not find it. It was too ridiculous for words, but the heavy curtain of snow still marred all visibility.

Without much difficulty, I managed to return to our operations room and a bit later tried again, but still without success. It was absurd, as the distance involved was so short that I simply had to strike the long barrack hut which housed the

Gordons.

Once again I walked out and this time I was determined to get something for our invalid. I was having no difficulty in finding my way back so I resolved to stay out until I located the Gordons' hut. I ploughed through the snow, plodding steadily forwards. I had to be careful as I had no desire to make contact with the barbed wire that enclosed the minefield surrounding the camp.

I knew that I had passed the hut and I looked up because the sky seemed a bit brighter. Suddenly, without any warning I found myself falling through space and my heart in my mouth, sank deeply down in the snow. Looking round I found what I had long lost, I could see the top part of the door at the end of the Gordons' hut. I had walked a curved path in the snow which had taken me right over the edge of the roof of the building and fallen through the enormous drift formed by its protected side. It was now obvious why I had been unable to find the hut on my previous excursions - I had been walking in a steady curve following the contour of the drift, not in a straight line at all!

With snow soaking my stockings and saturating my clothes, I slipped and ploughed my way thankfully to the door. I tried to hammer on the top part, but found that I was pounding on a thick sheet of ice. Starting to clear the snow from the base of the door, I kicked and hammered but with no apparent response. I began to think that perhaps the Gordons had left when the snow started.

Finally I heard a muffled "Och awa' wi' ya…" [Scottish dialect for "Go away!"]. I shouted for someone to come to the door. With someone pulling from the inside, I tore thin strips of ice from the doorposts and finally with a frightful jerk the door opened. Inside a Highlander was standing in comical long woollen underpants and a long-sleeved vest. He had a blanket slung around his shoulders to give protection from the cold and he eyed me through bleary, sleepy eyes. "What a-du wi' mon? Awa' hame to your bed."

I pointed out that we had no beds, and that one of our men was sick with hunger. Slowly the light dawned, and suddenly realising the plight we must have been in for the past two days and nights the whole hut went into action. The canny Scots knew what to do in this kind of weather, they hibernated. The snow had now almost stopped, and the morning sky had now taken on a lighter hue. Quickly preparing some cocoa and porridge on the coke stove in the centre of the room some willing Highlanders helped me carry the sustenance back to the CHL hut.

We clambered up the snowdrift the size of which was now clearly visible. Its immensity in no way impressed the Scotsmen, but I stared in amazement at the huge dune - like snowdrifts which stretched as far as the eye could see. Never in my life had I seen anything quite like it in the south.

Though it had now stopped snowing there was no way of getting down to the village, so we stayed put and awaited the next turn of events. After much argument and a host of promises to be carried out in the pub the next night, I managed to borrow two bicycle chains from the Gordon Highlanders. With these we got to work and repaired the transmitter turning gear so that when the line to Stanmore was eventually restored we could get on with the war.

On a memorable trip down to London, Jack graphically describes his experiences and shock at seeing Dally's home No. 39 Teesdale Street, bomb-damaged. He writes:

Having done one or two trips down south from Scotland, standing all the way in the icy corridors, I was more than grateful to be seated in the small, smoky, crowded compartment.

It wasn't until we approached London some hours later that the delays really started. The train constantly slowed to a walking pace before jolting to a halt. With the engine panting upfront, we waited time and time again until the train inched and squeaked its way jerkily forward. We could now hear the muted, distant racket of the London guns. By the sounds of things, an air raid was in full swing. Leaning out of the window and looking ahead, the sky and the clouds were bright with searchlights and the sky was pockmarked with the bursting of ack-

ack shells. The train now made a steady run and we prepared ourselves as it seemed that at any time now we would roll into King's Cross Station.

The roar of the guns was now deafening. We had crossed and recrossed a multitude of lines on the approaches to the station. We removed our luggage from the racks and prepared to disembark, when the train jerked to a sudden and violent halt. With the engine panting like a breathless dog we waited in silence until we heard the sound of footsteps beside the train.

"We shan't be long," shouted the railwayman "there's a landmine hanging over the signal gantry ahead. The train might shake it down, so we are sending for somebody to fix it.

"Wouldn't like a job like his," ventured the man sitting next to me. "Fancy fiddling with a land mine up a pole in the middle of the night!"

"He must be up the pole to take a job like that," suggested another.

We waited interminably, the fury of the guns had more or less abated but from time to time we heard the now familiar unsynchronised sound of the German aircraft motoring overhead. To me it seemed as if they were really staying over the London area to extend the period of the raid and the dislocation caused to the people of London. Just after 11 o'clock the "all clear" sounded. Quite unexpectedly we lurched forward and trundled into the familiar approach to the station platforms. I was hoping to make a dash for one of the last underground station trains and prepared for the long run.

As we entered the huge, dark and cathedral-like arch of the station, I could see that most of the small window panes overhead were smashed. Apart from the passengers leaving the train, the platform was practically deserted. I dashed along with my respirator and tin hat dancing on my rear. I reach the underground entrance and at high speed made my way down the stairs and along the tunnel to the waiting train where I was soon sitting in homely electric comfort. Reading the familiar advertisements on the walls it seemed to put life back into perspective. I made my way to St. Paul's station where I understood some elderly friends took nightly shelter.

As we paused at the various stations, I noted how the shelterers were already bedded down in their blankets and waiting for the last train to pass before dropping off to sleep. The platforms were crammed, with a little space near the edge for the passengers alighting from the trains. A small passage through the bodies allowed the transit of the passengers to and from the escalators.

At St Paul's I left the train and picked my way along the platform. I scanned the sea of bodies on both platforms and in the corridor. Travelling up the escalator I began my search on the next level. I was appalled at the large number of people sprawled, seemingly happily and comfortably over every inch of ground space. I myself would have put up with any danger rather than the indignity of sleeping under these conditions and that, of course was the attitude of most Londoners. For the most part it was mainly the elderly, the incapacitated and the children who were here. That is, those children who had not been evacuated.

It did not seem possible that just a few months before I had to use the tube station together with thousands of other commuters on their way to and from work. I found the sight very sad and dispiriting. After discovering that I had now missed the last train west to Ealing Broadway and home, I decided that rather than walk the long distant west, I would stay with my good friends in the East End of London, just a few miles away.

It was no use continuing my search in the now sleeping multitude, every step I took raised a sleepy grumble so I made my way up to the booking office level and then up the stairs to the street. "Better not go up there Air Force", cautioned a warden. "It's been pretty shaky tonight. Shaky or not, I urgently needed fresh air.

As I reached the street the air raid alert sounded once again. There were no signs nor sounds of aircraft or guns so I started to walk up Cheapside towards the Bank of England. I was really enjoying the brisk walk and fresh air. With arms swinging RAF style I made my way towards the east and a comfortable bed. Before I had made much progress I heard the menacing distant roar of a large number of aircraft. Though I thought, half-hopingly "Are they ours or theirs?" I knew they could only be "theirs". These thoughts were confirmed by the guns which once again opened up. As the raid seemed to be further west and I heard no sounds of dropping shrapnel, I did not trouble to put on my tin hat, it was such an effort to remount neatly on my respirator.

The crump of the bombs was almost a harmless sound compared to the intense racket of the guns. Trucks and lorries followed by an ambulance passed me on their way towards the West End. One small LDV driven by a woman with an elderly man sitting beside, screeched to a halt alongside me. "Come on cock. Give us a hand!" I forgot about the comfortable bed and climbed aboard the vehicle which promptly resumed its westward journey. As we approach High Holborn I saw smoking ruins. I did not realise that the bombs had dropped quite so close by. Thomas Wallis, the large store on my left, had obviously received a direct hit. We offloaded and inspected the building, the lintel of which was now hanging down miserably amongst the rubble.

The street was light with the multitude of searchlights reflected off the low cloud and rising smoke. It was indeed light enough to read the road that went off at an angle behind this corner building was itself blocked by enormous piles of rubble. Parking our truck in the main road a distance from the crumbling wall we climbed amongst the debris looking for signs of life. There was a little chance of anyone being trapped as nobody should have been in the vicinity of this building at the time.

A fall of masonry showered us with dust and filth. We moved along to the next building and the old man shouted that he had found somebody. From under a fallen coping stone, that had obviously been a doorway, the upturned palm of a hand was visible. Using spars of wood and bricks, we levered and raised the rubble until we could drag out the luckless victim. As he came out we found that he was an elderly gentleman in a well worn overcoat. He had possibly taken shelter in the doorway when the bombs crashed down. Lying there with a peaceful look on his face and his mouth wide open he looked almost as if he were about to snore. After rummaging through his pockets and making a note or two, presumably of identification, they placed him where he could be easily seen from the road and yet be protected from the traffic. For hours we moved from one pile of crumpled masonry to another but by now a small army of ARP [Air Raid Precautions] workers and vehicles had arrived in the area to search for anybody trapped in the wreckage.

Being a business centre there were fortunately not many people around during the time of the raid. In Farringdon and the surrounding district however, there had been a large number of casualties and deaths. After a dawn cup of cocoa at a mobile canteen, my friends dropped me off at Liverpool Street station and I started to walk towards Bethnal Green in the company of a soldier returning home on compassionate leave. He was heading for Canrobert Street and I for Teesdale Street.

As we marched we talked about anything but the bombing. Walking up Bethnal Green Road the damage caused by the night's bombing was very evident. As I left my soldier friend and turned left into Teesdale Street, I noticed with a shock that a block of five double storied terrace houses had disappeared, leaving an ominous gap. The bomb blast had squirted in its unpredictable way along the street, smashing the windows and blowing the doors off the hinges and doing damage in the most unexpected places.

Almost opposite the demolished houses was the house I intended to visit, number 39. All its windows were smashed and the tiles had been skimmed off the roof. I approached the front door with trepidation hoping that nobody I knew had been in the house at the time of the incident. I stepped over the front step and saw that the heavy front door had been blown bodily right up the long passage where it rested on some stairs. Though there was dust everywhere, nothing else seemed to have been damaged.

I looked in all the rooms on the ground floor. They were empty so I shouted loudly "Anybody at home?" and a muffled voice answered me from upstairs. I tore up the stairs fearing the worst. I found the door of one of the bedrooms lying half across the bed used by one of the younger male members of the household. Gently lifting it up I found myself looking into a pair of tired eyes.

"You okay, Maurice?" I enquired. [Maurice was one of Dell's younger brothers].

"Yes," he replied with some annoyance. "Can't you let a man sleep?" I gently lowered the door back into position. This was a typical London attitude. The damage had been done, it would be cleared up in due course, but at this moment sleep was far more important. This was just one of the many inconveniences brought about by Hitler and his gang.

I went downstairs, took off my greatcoat and looking for a screwdriver, I started to put the big door back in its place before the old lady returned home. It is hard to describe to anyone apart from an East Ender, just what pride of place the street door had been in the life of a cockney housewife. Only a short time ago the door knocker, the letterbox and the doorknob were weekly subjected to a vigorous shine worthy of a battleship. The front doorstep was scrubbed white and the little window over the door was fitted weekly with a clean lace curtain as a gesture of defiance against the London soot. The front door was always the housewife's challenge to the world. To find this edifice off and deposited amongst the rubble would have been a sad blow to the morale of the old people. I was determined to get it back in place before they came back from the shelter.

Finding the door extremely heavy to handle, I went upstairs and tipped Maurice out of bed. Locating a dressing gown, he looked about him in wonder. Going downstairs, he helped me to find some screws and tools. We plugged the holes and more by good luck than judgement, we managed to get the door back in place. Admittedly, it needed a certain amount of persuasion to make it perform its normal function but the status quo had been restored just as the first arrival appeared. It was one of the younger members of the family who had been on duty as an ARP runner. The man of the house [Isaac Bernard] then appeared after a night's duty as an air raid warden. He greeted me with the cheerful but cynical crack of the time, "Lucky we've got an Air Force".

Shortly after, the lady of the house [Dally's mother, Mina] appeared from St. Paul's tube station with the youngest member of the family [Frankie]. Laden with blankets and a hamper holding the night's rations, they entered the house. Graciously ignoring the rubble, with not a word about the raid the night before, or the houses across the road which had disappeared with their occupants during the night, her first words to the gathered menfolk were, "Who wants a nice cup of tea?" Whilst tea was being prepared, a concerted attack was made on the mess. Feeling very much better after a strong cup of tea and a good wash, I returned to one of the undamaged bedrooms for a few hours much needed sleep. As I sank into the down-filled pillows I thought of all the uncomfortable places I had been sleeping of late. My reverie was interrupted by strident instructions to the household by the lady of the house.

"Maurice, dad, and I will clear up, you get ready for work!"

"Frank, wash now and get ready for school."

"Julius, take your ARP bicycle out of the passage!"

Hitler or no Hitler, normality has been restored, "Dad and I will clear up, you get ready for work!"

The efforts of the scheming villains of Wilhelmstrasse were all to nothing. I had every right to be proud of my association with the indomitable Londoners. In any case, I was born in the very heart of London, in fact the City of London Maternity Hospital to be precise. Just how Cockney could you get? With these comforting thoughts on London pride, I fell asleep.

While Jack was in Rosehearty he had to organise for a practice defence from German invasion.

In his letters he writes about the mock invasion. It reads like something out of the BBC series Dad's Army. In fact the "enemy" were the Home Guard.

This light-hearted "bit of fun" must have been a welcome relief from the depressing situation around him.

Jack's writing is humorously graphic in detail and he even manages to transliterate the strong Scottish accent of his men. He also seems to have adopted Scottish expressions himself, even introducing words, such as "scunnered" (fed up), "ken" (know) and "binding" (RAF slang; complaining).

21.8. 41

Incidentally we're having a private personal invasion tonight so I'll give you the gen on how we get on in my next letter; and I'll be writing it tomorrow not next month; that'll shake you. The invasion will be attempted by a crack Home Guard unit who have taken every station so far. I must now prepare a reception for them so cheerio for now

Yours,

Jack

37 Pitsligo St.,
Rosehearty

23 Aug. 41

My Dear Dally,

We have just finished our private invasion. I haven't had so much fun for a long time.

We, that is the people being invaded, had a good time. The Home Guard had a horrible time. Their main job was to crawl along wet fields covered in camouflage.

Cows left plenty of natural camouflage about but it doesn't half stink.

The first party captured included the H.G commander: was he scunnert!!! [Scottish dialect: "fed up"]

I had arranged field telephones in all the strategic positions and a small radio telephone on a tower which commanded a view of the (H.G.) [Home Guard] initial start.

The telephones were well camouflaged in trench posts and we received the "gen" as soon as the invaders spread out to invade.

They didn't do much invading because they were theoretically wiped out by the Lewis guns as soon as they were reported.

We captured seventy-five Home Guardsmen including their commander and two 2nd lieutenants.

One of my men, a motor transport driver from Glasgow, captured twenty HG twerps.

He was out at our south outpost when he saw some cows rather nervously hopping about. Naturally he became suspicious and eventually sighted some H.G. twerps crawling along with long grass tied to their posteriors and keeping their noses to the ground.

He approached them on the other side of a dyke [hedge] and presently he could hear them "Shushing" and telling each other to keep quiet.

When they got level with him he bobbed up on the top of the dyke and watched them; they were mooing like cows and calling each other with birdcalls.

Anyway he got cheesed with watching these twerps crawling in the cow's stuff, so he frightened them by yelling out in Glaswegian "Dinna shush you've had it!" He was a trifle shocked when about fifteen H.G's got up with their hands up. The next telephone post reported this and a mobile section was sent out to bring them in.

Personally I didn't do any "capturing". I had arranged the "signals", and was acting as "defence command" and control. Receiving the invaders line of approach and counteracting it. I found it very interesting and so did the umpires. The umpires included regular army Majors, two Captains, an Air Commodore and a Wing Commander. Sorry, Lord Saltoun as well.

The army Guard Commander, Major Ross, said it was a perfect defence and wanted to know details of the signals system.

After the invasion had flopped, about midnight I started giving him the gen on my own signals of defence.

He was extremely enthusiastic and has invited me over to his place a little way inland to get some standard plans drawn up for minimum radio establishment of army stations defence.

That night we had cocoa around the Guard Room stove, and did it taste good.

The tabs and crowns [people in higher ranks according to their uniform] made me rather sick but I managed to put up with them until about two o/c in the morning, when we all came back to Rosehearty for bed.

That's enough tripe. I don't think somehow, you will find it over interesting; what with my rotten writing and bad grammar, you'll find it rather binding.......................

yours,

Jack.

Jack in Highland garb, 1941.

Chapter Four: Jack breaks the law

In *The Wizard War* Jack tells a fascinating story about a visit he made to the station at Dyce Aerodrome.

With my Scots conspirator, William Mackenzie, I made a trip to the fire station at Dyce Aerodrome. Flying at this time from the aerodrome were the Hurricanes of the Czech Air Force Squadron. In the local pub we made contact with some of the Czech pilots, one of whom was a flight commander. With a little prodding this man was made to pour out his heart on the stupidity of the RAF High Command who sent them out to combat German aircraft which had already landed at their home bases. He went to great pains to assure me that a thing like this would never have happened in Czechoslovakia, where, co-incidentally, the beer was much better.

Though we were in RAF uniform he knew nothing of our special work, and we led him to believe that we were radio-telephony mechanics stationed near Fraserburgh. In a sly manner, we let slip that from our radio-telephony hut we often saw enemy aircraft flitting around the sea with plenty of time for the Czechs to carry out their interceptions, that is, of course, if we could have used the radio telephone. I said it was unthinkable, that we in our lowly capacity could ever interfere with the slow, rumbling machine of Fighter Command. This produced a truly Slavonic explosion.

"Despite the fact," I said, "that we have access to the forward relay transmitter that controls their aircraft in our little compound, it is of course unthinkable that we should interfere with the transmissions." He now became quite excited and said in his own brand of English, "What about it? To hell with Fighter Command! You help us shoot down the Germans!"

At high-speed I then poured out the plan I had in mind. This man was no fool, and he realised that the whole meeting was a put-up job, but as it might help eradicate some of the enemy bombers, he was with us right up to the hilt.

We arranged for a special code word for "scramble" to be passed to the set control room at Dyce. This was effected by passing the word on our radar plotting line to Schoolhill CH station in Aberdeen. They in turn passed it through their radio telephone line connected to Dyce operations room. When the code word reached the sector operations room the Czechs were somehow to arrange for a group of Hurricanes to get airborne quickly, ostensibly on a "cross country exercise", and under the usual sector control. Once airborne, the aircraft were to come into our directional area. On reaching a reasonable height, we could see them perfectly on our radar well to the south. We had agreed on codewords for the main rocky headlands and villages in this area. We were in business.

I fixed a GPO-type 14 switch as a

transmit/receive switch for controlling the powerful 1130 1VHS transmitter which was situated in our compound. With the aid of a field telephone temporarily borrowed from the guardroom and connected to the transmitter modulation line, at the throw of a switch, I could transmit to the fighter aircraft. My messages were short and sweet and must have been more than puzzling to the men keeping the logbooks at Dyce. "Apples, angels three", meant enemy aircraft in the vicinity of Fraserburgh were at 3,000 feet. The fighters then had deadly accurate position information on hostile aircraft at that time and no longer relied on the delayed and inaccurate information from Dyce sector operations room.

After a few false starts when the code word "scramble" for some reason or other did not get correctly interpreted at Dyce sector operations room, the Czechs arranged for a spy to be available in the "Ops room" throughout daylight hours to ensure that a section of fighter aircraft was scrambled promptly upon the receipt of the secret order. I, in turn, arranged with Bill MacKenzie that one of us would always be on duty throughout the daylight hours, even if we were again on duty that night. We were all dedicated to our work and little else mattered.

When I came down from the station, worn out, tired, frozen and flagged, I could always rely on Mrs Chrissie Buchan to have a pot of hot bros [oat porridge] on the stove. I am sure Robbie

Burns and Lord Pitsligo, that great Scottish Nationalist, would both have turned in their graves if they could have seen how the Scottish women spared nothing in the efforts to maintain us Sassenachs.

Our scheme was almost immediately successful with the interception of a Heinkel III carried out after the first of our scramble signals had got through. This enemy aircraft got away but at least one of our Hurricanes had made contact.

A few days later another Heinkel was damaged and crash-landed on the rocks west of Rosehearty. A week or two after that a Junkers 88 was forced down into the sea off Fraserburgh and the occupants were fortunate enough to get into their dinghy. I imagine their luck ended there, because some of our local Gordon Highlanders set out in a rowing boat to greet them; fortunately I did not hear the end of the story.

Perhaps we, by reason of our new-found success had incurred the displeasure of the third Luftwaffe fleet because they delivered the first really damaging attack on Fraserburgh causing many casualties in this picturesque Scottish fishing harbour. This dock area could be regarded, even at this early juncture of the war, as a military target, because the first of the secret magnetic minesweepers of the highly specialised design were being manufactured in the small shipyards.

It was inevitable that Jack's daring if brilliant scheme for the early interception of enemy aircraft would be uncovered.

The night of the big raid ended badly for me. Sometime after midnight a young administrative officer of the station had either stumbled over some of our wires to the transmitter in the radio telephone hut, or somebody had told him of my machinations for aircraft interception. Coming to the wrong conclusions, he had sent a truck into Fraserburgh and got the military police to locate me, whereupon I was brought back to the station under escort as a spy. Hitler, I am sure, would have appreciated the services of the Jewish spy!

I managed to obtain permission to sleep in my own billet for the night; the next day, however, our little station wore an air of anxious expectancy and most of the chaps would not speak to me. [what he had presumably failed to consider was the possibility that rather than being credited with making a significant contribution to Britain's safety he would receive quite other treatment.] A signal arrived from the south, and I was ordered to proceed to London under close arrest. After collecting my small kit, the military escort and I managed to board the afternoon train from Fraserburgh to Aberdeen. From there we transferred to the Aberdonian, my escort close on my tail. The interminable, cold, uncomfortable journey from Aberdeen that night was made all the more miserable as my service police escort refused to indulge in any conversation with me. His silence gave me plenty of time to contemplate all my sins and misdeeds. By the time we had reached the suburbs of London, I was convinced that I would ultimately end up in the Tower!

We arrived at Kings Cross Station tired, cold and hungry in the early hours of the morning and made our way to one of the workmen's early trains which took us north to Oxenden House in Leighton Buzzard, headquarters of 60 Group. This was the most sacrosanct of all the citadels in the RAF radar branch. Here sat the pundits within their secret empire achieving Herculean technological feats in the building of new radar stations, and the training of the technicians and operators to man them. A visit to this old mansion, in its lovely grounds was, for the radar man at that time, very much as a visit to Mecca would be to a devout Muslim.

We marched across the yard to the huge front door, where an armed service policeman requested the documents authorising our admittance to the Holy of Holies. With my faithful guardian we were made to wait outside the office in a cold, dark corridor for the arrival of an RAF officer. After a depressingly long wait he arrived, and re-directed us to the office of another more senior officer as he knew nothing at all about us. By now my morale had been reduced to a very low ebb.

The new man arrived, and we were ushered into his presence by a Warrant Officer carrying a large and ominous-looking file under his arm. This, no doubt, was a list of all my offences to date against the RAF and would include: unauthorised modifications to RDF equipment; interference with very high frequency communications to fighter aircraft; endangering the lives of flying personnel; passing on unauthorised communications along secret telephone wires. These were but a few! I stood uncomfortably while the Flight Lieutenant studied the file, wearing what I thought was an extremely stern expression. I watched his facial expression change as he continued to study the script before him in complete silence. I prepared for the worst.

His first remark caught me quite off guard.

"Well," he said, "how did you do it?"

Before I had a chance to answer he asked, "Have you had any breakfast?"

"No, sir," I replied. "We have come straight from King's Cross Station and we did not stop for food."

He spoke to the Warrant Officer.

"Please organise us some tea."

"But sir, it's a bit early!" came the reply.

"Well, please use your good offices with the tea swindle. [RAF term for tea trolley]"

And, to my escort still hovering around,

"Would you please leave us alone, as this matter does not concern you."

The Warrant Officer brought in some very welcome tea and again left the room.

When we were alone, he said "Right! Pull up your chair and let's see how you went about it."

Gradually I explained how, with a minimum of interference with RAF procedure, I had managed to place fighters in a reasonable position for the intersection of the enemy bombers.

"Look" said the officer, "I know nothing at all about all these contraventions. I am only interested in our ability to dispose of the Hun. If I were you I would forget about details, but since you've engaged yourself on the radar and navigational problems of aircraft interception, how would you like to work on the GCI?"

"The what, sir?" I queried.

"Ground Control of Interception. This is a new type of station doing precisely what you have described. The first of these is still in the process of development, but nevertheless, almost operational."

I was overjoyed at the prospect of going to work on this problem which had interested me since long before the war. As it transpired, I stayed with this type of station in all its various shapes and forms as it developed, both in Great Britain and the Middle East.

Returning to Scotland for a short time, I waited for my official posting to the Royal Aircraft Establishment at Farnborough. This short return trip to Scotland proved to be the most interesting as I witnessed a radar phenomenon that changed the whole scientific world's conception of the performance of very high-frequency radio transmissions.

It happened on an evening radar watch. Quite suddenly, enormous signals came echoing from way out over the North Sea. The careful checks I made proved that these responses were echoes off the Hardanger Mountains of Norway, somewhere around 300 miles away from us. This meant that the impossible was happening. At that time, the whole radio fraternity was convinced that these very high-frequency radio transmissions were like light and travelled in a straight line, to be lost out in space. The fantastically strong signal we were now receiving from the mountains meant that our one and a half metre transmissions could in fact - and were - being bent around the curvature of the earth and giving us the reflections of these mountains which were, of course, in enemy territory. Realising the importance of this discovery, and its possible usefulness as a navigational aid, I sat up all night plotting the signals and the next day sent a mass of tracings and maps up to Dr Bowen, the Bawdsey radar pioneer who was then hard at work in Kirkwall in the Orkney Islands. Needless to say, he was delighted, as the fact that this kind of phenomena could take place suggested a precision bombing aid.

My stay in Scotland was all too short, and when I took my leave of my host and hostess, Mr and Mrs John Buchan, I felt as if I were leaving home.

Rosehearty from the radar station

Generally, the little village of Rosehearty had been very fortunate to date and spared the violence of war. Apart from the shock one morning of finding some German magnetic mines that had been washed ashore in the village, there had been no bombing. When I left, I pleaded with Mrs Buchan to quickly take cover in the small central granite block cottage of the house if the sound of low aircraft engines were suddenly heard. The typical granite, square Aberdonian cottage filled the heart of her large rambling house, which was composed mainly of wooden outbuildings. My last words to her were to take cover under the bed in the granite section and not to delay when the aircraft sounded very low. She promised to take immediate cover as I had directed. Within a short time of my departure for Farnborough in the summer, it happened. A sharp air raid was carried out on the small village killing a large number of people. A bomb wrecked number 37 Pitsligo Street, but Mrs Buchan and her daughters Jeanne and Evelyn had heeded my warning and were found under the bed of the wrecked house, luckily quite unhurt.

On 9 February 1942 my mother Dally noted in her diary, "Received a very sad letter from Mrs Buchan telling me how she has been bombed out."

I am still in touch with Evelyn's son Alan Leel, and although he was not yet born at the time, the family are understandably very grateful for this advice.

Chapter Five: The natives were hostile

"We don't want you military down by here," the rather aged postmistress was most insistent.

"We've 'ad no bombs and we don't want none."

"I'm only asking you to tell me the whereabouts of Soarmill Farm." I pleaded.

"There be no such place and don't waste our time; we've got a lot of work to do."

I had arrived in South Devon to build a day and night fighter station to help protect Bristol and other western areas from the enemy bombers based across the Channel. The work was intensely secret so I couldn't tell anyone, and I could of course tell nobody of my problems. Armed with a map and a six-figure pin point [grid reference], I knew the site of the station was somewhere on the headland known as Start Point. This is a large bulge in the South Devon coast near Plymouth, the closest we could get to the Luftwaffe across the Channel.

There was no doubt about it, the natives were hostile, my father writes.

Though it was well into 1941, the war had not yet reached the sunny South West of England. Here, quite illegally, one could still buy rich Devonshire cream and whole legs of ham, whilst the people in the town had two ounces of bacon per person per week, if that.

I had my duty to do and time was running out.

I was tired and hungry and anxious to locate my new station.

"Right!" I sighed, "Where will I find the village policeman?"

"Oh, I don't know. He is around somewhere maybe."

A young girl behind the counter piped up, "He lives in the cottage just up the end of the street."

The elderly postmistress gave the girl a withering glance.

"Many thanks," I said and took my leave. As I retired from the post office the elderly lady dived for the telephone. Perhaps that is why, when I got to the policeman's house he was not at home and his wife seemed to have no idea where he could possibly be. This was indeed strange, as the beautiful village of Malborough in South Devon had but one street, and it would be quite difficult for anyone to get lost, especially a six-foot policeman.

Malborough, Higher Town, a Devonshire Water Carrier.

Dear Dally,

I thought you might be interested in a picture of my new abode.

There are four super-cinemas, swimming-pool and skating-rink, but not in this part of the world.

Jack.

Miss A. Bernard,
39, Teesdale St.,
London,
E. 2.

Jack is billeted in Alma House, Malborough when he is sent to Bolt Head in Devon. This is a postcard Jack sent to Dell. On the picture he indicated where his lodging was – 'My Palace'. Reproduced from an original Frith's Series postcard.

He later took over the Cottage Hotel, Hope Cove as a billet for the staff, and had the honeymoon suite, but occasionally still used Alma House, as it was closer to the radar station; a brisk walk in fact. His humour can be appreciated by what he wrote. Reproduced from an original Frith's Series postcard.

Jack describes spending the morning walking over the Bolt Head region of the Start Point looking for the new station.

> Standing on top of a large headland, with the aid of a compass and map, I knew I must be on the spot where the RAF station Bolt Head, should have been, but all I could see was grass and much evidence of recent occupation of this meadow by many cows.
>
> From Exeter I had been told that this was my new station. Standing on top of the headland and looking out to sea, I definitely fixed my position, as in the distance across the Salcombe Estuary I could see the 360-foot mast of CH radar station West Prawle, one of the earliest Chain Home radar stations which had done such a wonderful job a few months previously in the Battle of Britain.
>
> I returned to the post office and booked a trunk call to RAF station Exeter, approximately seventy miles north. I made contact with a disinterested orderly duty clerk and told him of my predicament without divulging any secret information. He informed me, in no uncertain terms, that he could not have cared less!
>
> This, then, was my introduction to No.10 group, Fighter Command. I had now left the fantastically efficient embrace of No. 60 group and was doing my first job of work for this group of Fighter Command. They had started nicely by posting me to a non-existent station. No doubt it was a station that had been marked on

the map by some senior officer somewhere during a planning discussion, but, he had omitted to state that it was a proposed station and not an actual one: worse was to follow, this was only the beginning.

It had started to rain heavily and I was feeling thoroughly miserable when the girl in the post office informed me, with great excitement, that another crowd of RAF boys had just arrived and were waiting for me at the station [Kingsbridge Station]. I trudged to the station and, true enough, when I arrived there were some thirty men waiting for me. A cook, motor transport drivers, general duties men, in fact the complement of a whole RAF station, except there was no station! Keeping them on the platform and under the shelter, I could hear the mumbles and grumbles of revolt. I did not tell them that we had no place to go to and that we were nobody's babies. [unwanted orphans].

The stationmaster, an old sweat wearing his ribbons from the First World War, came to my rescue.

"Look," he said, "The ladies of the village don't trust airmen; not that we've had any military personnel here as yet, but they have locked up their daughters, their goats and everything else. There are no more trains out of the station tonight, so the best thing you can do is take your lads and march down to Hope Cove, a small seaside village about three miles away. There's where you will find a few hotels and at least get under cover for the night."

I formed the lads up, made them put on their capes, and with their kit bags on their backs, we marched out of the station and down a long, winding, narrow, muddy lane towards Hope Cove. We marched and marched. The rain now was very heavy, and the men tired. I called halts for rest more and more frequently. The lane grew narrower and narrower, and the rain made visibility nil.

To make matters worse it was now getting dark. When I had almost given up hope I saw, for a brief moment, the eaves of a large house in the distance. This was the first sign of civilisation since we had started our march. Splashed by the red mud, sopping wet, steaming and tired, we slithered and slipped down the steep road and to the front of the house I had seen from the road. It was some form of inn. In front of the hotel was a large drive and yard, and with a semblance of military order, I lined the men up outside. After trying to make myself look respectable, I entered the magnificent, panelled lounge with its huge fireplace aglow with blazing logs.

The owner, a Mr Halliday, was a grand fellow and after hearing my sad story and taking one look at my bedraggled and miserable squad, he ordered us indoors at once. As the red squishy, sticky mud entered the lounge, my heart skipped a beat, as I was sure the proprietor would surely change his mind. He took us into the warm spacious kitchen of the hotel, where my men spread themselves out and dried off their saturated clothes. I then made them clear up the mess we had made and assist with some other general chores in the hotel. At least we had a roof over our heads for the night and in no time the lads were stuffing themselves with wonderful food; food worthy of this most magnificent hotel. Though at the time I did not know it, this beautiful place was to become our home for some time to come, and it became the headquarters of our night fighter control station that was to cost the Luftwaffe dearly in men and machines.

I was up at dawn next morning. It had stopped raining and the view down towards the sea and around the cove was thrilling. I had never seen a more beautiful place. Blue skies reflected in the blue waters, framed by the delicate golden-brown sands, completed the wonderful scene. Almost beneath the hotel, but in the sea, there were some small fishing boats; the fishermen were pulling in their baskets of crayfish and lobster. After the last two years of work in the frozen north and the trials and tribulations of the Battle of Britain, this was like heaven, a heaven on earth.

Our new and apparently temporary home was called the Cottage Hotel, and even after just a few hours in this wonderful place, I began to feel more like tackling the problems ahead.

The Cottage Hotel still exists today, and is a popular venue for Devon holidays. As a family we have visited it several times. It truly is a beautiful little cove where the hotel is situated. One can also travel up to Bolt Head to see a plaque, which was unveiled in 1999 mentioning Jack's achievements.

I cannot really imagine how wonderful it must have been for a twenty-two-year-old boy from the East End to have been billeted in this beautiful hotel. How fortunate for him that the postings were that way round! Imagine going from picturesque, sunny luxurious Devon, back to Mrs Buchan's boarding house in the Frozen North!

Jack's room with the sunken bath is still there, but not offered as accommodation.

My father always told me that, Archimedes-like, he always had his best ideas in the bath. (A trait I have inherited!) That sunken bath in the beautiful honeymoon suite was certainly very inspirational…To get back to Jack on his first morning at Hope Cove…

After a delicious breakfast, and with the permission of the proprietor, I phoned Exeter airport/aerodrome in an effort to discover where and how we were to establish a new station. I drew a complete blank. In desperation I rang the South Devon headquarters of my old organisation at Ashburton. Here I was promised immediate help. I gave the hotel number, Galmpton 213. In the event of any information becoming available, they could contact me at the hotel.

The whole matter was complicated by the fact that I could make no reference to the type of technical equipment I was expecting. At each end of the line, we were both intensely security conscious; as usual 60 Group allowed no grass to grow under its feet, and by midday it had arranged for an army telephone unit to lay on an emergency telephone line to the point which I directed. With my limited positional knowledge, I chose a spot which I thought would be best for the location of the radar station we intended to install. This, then, was the first hurdle. The telephone was simply placed in a small wooden box in the centre of a field so recently occupied by a large herd of cows.

The nature of the terrain was that of an inverted saucer, and certainly not the ideal site for the type of radar station where accurate height reading was required. It was quite obvious, however, that no more suitable site was available in the vicinity. With a box of sandwiches, carefully prepared by mine host in the hotel and a flask of tea, I sat on the ground sheet and kept a lonely vigil by the telephone.

I was feeling thoroughly miserable after a heavy downpour, when in mid-afternoon my 60 Group headquarters came through on the telephone with glad news that the wheels were turning, and that sometime tomorrow I could expect the arrival of my equipment.

To assist in my rapid installation of this important defensive station, the radio equipment had been installed in large Crossley motor lorries at the factory. On arrival at the radar site, these convoys would be lined up, interleading cables connected and in a short time the radar station would be in full operation.

This new type of convoy consisted of an operations room vehicle, complete with radar receiver, and navigational aids. Another vehicle was complete with a two-ton radio transmitter, a trailer carrying the 15 KVA diesel electrical power supply system and an aerial trailer. To complete the set there was, of course, a workshop vehicle with everything one would require for the assembly of the aerial system at the station.

In the village of Malborough I kept a man on permanent watch duty, waiting and praying for the eventual arrival of our convoy.

Two days and nights went by and we were still waiting. On one of these evenings we saw and heard a prolonged and heavy air raid on Plymouth, a few miles west along the coast. In Hope Cove, however, everything was peaceful. Apart from the distant echoing racket of the anti-aircraft guns we were not in any way disturbed.

At midday the following day, my guard in Malborough village phoned from the post office, and excitedly proclaimed the arrival of our convoy. Climbing aboard the leading vehicle he led the convoy out to my location. After hearty introductions all round, the convoy was lined up for operations, in such a way that its blind spot would cause the least interference with future operations.

Typical GCI convoy. Everything needed to set up the station was loaded onto Crossley lorries and transported to the chosen site. GCI (Ground Control Interception) was a radar station with a small airstrip with its own fighter aircraft. It was for these personnel that Jack had to find billets and he also had to set up the radar station using the equipment on the lorries.

I set out the station orderly room in the transmitter vehicle of the convoy. The men worked like slaves setting up the equipment and all the facilities. As usual, 60 Group came to the rescue, even though it was not their pigeon, and by that evening our equipment was already operating. This allowed us to have a grandstand radar-wise view of another sharper attack on Plymouth in which a lot of damage and loss of life occurred.

Without our telephone lines to the radio telephony transmitters and to the operations room in Exeter we were powerless to intervene. I could only watch the comings and goings of the enemy bombers, which were quite unmolested apart from the heavy local anti-aircraft fire. This attack seemed to spur the authorities into action and the next day the AFS [Air Force Service/Auxiliary Fire Service] telephone men put in an appearance, and by that evening we had two private and secret lines through to the sector operations station at Exeter airport.

I had worked all the previous night calibrating the front of our planned position indicator tube. This 12-inch circular tube gave us the positioning of all the aircraft, and on it I had to draw in Indian ink, the map with the military group reference indications so that the plots of the enemy bombers and fighters could be read off, and, of course, passed to sector, as well as acted upon by ourselves.

Despite the fact that we had to use the VHF wireless transmitter receivers at Exeter for controlling our fighters, we were in business. With technical stores borrowed from Exminster GCI [Ground Control Interception] a station which was nearer to Exeter than we were, we went through the operations of night fighter interceptions and controlling in broad daylight. There were inevitable snags and breakdowns, and inadequacies, but within a week we were calibrated for height finding and eagerly awaiting our first customers.

After the rigours of life in the Frozen North, to be stationed in South Devon was sublime. The whole area from Exeter, the hometown of our sister station Exminster, situated just outside the town on the river Exe, to Plymouth a few miles to our west was studded with names that in peace time, I had only seen on travel brochures. Torquay, Dartmouth, Salcombe, Thurlston and Hope Cove; really the holiday places of the upper set. To be working in sunshine under a blue sky, rather than digging down through the snow to feed our diesel electric supply with oil, was indeed a contrast. Life in this part of the world reminded me very much of my pre-war holidays on the Isle of Wight. The beautiful coves and sandy beaches made wonderful playgrounds for our non-working hours. One could go for walks along the seafront avoiding, of course, the long narrow, carefully marked mined sections on the beach. The war, however, during those walks seemed incredibly remote.

My periods off duty were, however, very few and far between. Our field on Soar Mill Farm, so recently occupied by other meadow ladies, was now a smartly turned-out little radar station complete with orderly and guard rooms and all the other requirements of an RAF station. Although we had no visitors from the German Air Force, I was extremely worried about the camouflage situation. With the aid of the army stationed at Kingsbridge, a few miles away, we managed to drag some sacking over various critical points to disguise the general appearance of the station, and to ensure that when viewed in silhouette, it would not resemble a group of buildings and vehicles.

Hurricanes and Spitfires which cooperated with us in our daily control exercises, were now using the grass strips beside the GCI as a temporary landing field. After a short lapse, gangs of labourers arrived and laid out the mesh for the two longish runways, strategically set out to take advantage of the prevailing winds. The idea was to develop a prototype defence unit consisting of radar, aircraft and servicing personnel. Once the operational and administrational snags had been overcome and the minimum personnel establishment had been decided upon, this unit would be replicated and sent en bloc to trouble spots overseas.

All this, however, was in the vague and distant future. We were still in England and not at all certain that Hitler wouldn't find some way of resurrecting operation 'Sea Lion', the invasion of England which had been put off from the previous season. In 1941 Kesselring's successful airborne invasion of Crete and Greece had taken place. The speed with which these operations had been carried out left us no room or reason for apathy. As quickly as possible we built up the air defences of South Western England.

Anyone who has been lucky enough to have been a guest at the Cottage Hotel will understand when I say that the appointments of this place were practically perfect. My room was the Blue Room. It had a blue motif: blue curtains, blue blankets, blue eiderdowns and even a blue tiled private bathroom, with a blue sunken bath.

The hotel kitchen was modern and first-rate and the panelled lounge with its large fireplace was a joy to behold.

A small bar had been built up from the timbers of a four master schooner, the 'Herzogin Cecile', that had gone aground off Hope Cove a few years prior to our taking up occupation. The whole of a small cabin, complete with benches, low tables, wall timber and portholes had been perfectly re-assembled. With model scenery lit up by small lamps outside the portholes, one might easily have been at sea. After a few drinks when one's equilibrium became somewhat disturbed, the illusion became complete.

There were no guides or precedents for this new type of radar system, and for most of the station's initiation, I worked night and day. Fortunately for me, I had found two old sweats from the First World War to take care of and set up the domestic camp at the Cottage Hotel.

Mack Shave, though twice my age, was the younger of these men. During the First World War he had been in the army and had developed the art of scrounging to the nth degree. He would take our Crossley workshop truck to Exeter, and without all the usual paperwork that bogged down us ordinary mortals in the RAF, he would come back with all our store requirements. His non-service methods of obtaining our service requisites usually got him into spots of bother, but one thing is certain, without his "organizing" ability the station would have taken months to have become established.

In his letter to Dally written on 26 December 1941 Jack writes:

Fighter C[ommand] have decided to give us an extremely important job which involves the use of tons more apparatus. Same tripe is now turning up in wagons and being NCOIC [Non-Commissioned Officer in Charge] I must ensure that nothing is knocked off, that nobody starts are poking their noses where they don't belong and what is most important, that some extremely dangerous apparatus is correctly wired up.

The latter is reputed to be my true job but I have also got to act as disciplinary, defence and technical officer. I don't mind work when it doesn't interfere too much with my personal existence but if they don't turn it down soon this public servant will be unserviceable.

The other aid was our storeman, Leslie Ferriday and although one would never believe it, a parson's son. During the First World War, he was in the Royal Navy, and from what I managed to extract from him, the Royal Navy was more than glad when the war was eventually over, as it enabled them to dispense with his services! His work was excellent, and under his control we were never short of the thousand and one items we consumed in the radio operations room at an alarming rate. Les, despite his middle age enjoyed practical jokes, but on one occasion he excelled himself and nearly gave me and most of South Western command, a heart attack.

One of his youthful duties in the dim and distant past was to be bellringer in his father's church. He knew all the tricks of the church bell ringing trade, and he longed to demonstrate to all and sundry his ability on the bells of the beautiful Marlborough church [locals I have spoken to, think it may have been Galmpton church]. Of course, this was out of the question. The ringing of church bells, which had been silent since the outbreak of war, was a long-awaited warning of parachutists and the German invasion. Without further instructions and upon hearing church bells, the area army commanders were to order all their units to stand to. The Home Guard would have to rush on duty and take up their appointed posts. The beaches would be patrolled, guns manned and the whole anti - invasion patrol machinery brought into operation. This vast defensive move hinged solely upon one thing, the church bells tolling across the countryside.

At various times Les had suggested that Christmas without bells, was not Christmas. This Christmas, 1941, rain or shine, he had boasted in the pub, he intended to ring the church bells at Malborough. This had been reported to my friend, the one and only village policeman. He approached me and unofficially told me to warn Mr Ferriday to behave himself and leave the church bells alone. I warned Leslie, in quiet discussion, over a pint of beer, of the machinery which came into action upon the ringing of these bells. I pointed out that the whole of the countryside as far as Plymouth, including the naval base (where he had once been stationed), would be roused if he carried out his threat, also that the army commander in the area would undoubtedly have him lodged in the glasshouse [military prison] for the rest of his life, if he did anything so idiotic. Les, who despite his age respected my gentlemanly requests, agreed and said yes of course he would never do anything quite so silly.

It was the 24 December I had returned to the hotel after a hard day's work, for some food and intended, after a rest, to go out to the station, the duty watch for Christmas Eve. I sat in the small office behind the hotel lounge. It was now quite dark, and I was attending to some station paperwork before retiring for a short rest. There was a splendid His Master's Voice radiogram in the tiny office and I had purchased a record of the popular hit of the time, the Warsaw Concerto (the music from the film Dangerous Moonlight) I decided to switch on the gramophone and listen to this rather pleasant concerto before going up for my rest.

Suddenly, I could scarcely believe my ears. I heard the church bells of Malborough tolling across the fields. I rushed to the door to make sure. There was no doubt, the bells were ringing out across the countryside, loud and clear. I quickly rang the radar station. Yes, they had heard the bells, but though they had two aircraft under control, there was no report of any invasion or any other enemy activity. We kept the line open in case a flash of news came through from the sector operations room at Exeter. In my heart of hearts, however, I knew that Les had carried out his deadly promise. I didn't dare think of all the panic it had caused, and on Christmas Eve too. I almost hoped it really was an invasion and sat down at the phone and kept in contact with the non-commissioned officer in charge of the watch at Bolt Head Station.

After a while there was a sudden pounding of boots in the yard behind the office. Les came flying through the back door. "They're after me!" he gasped. "The cops. They're after me!"

He dived under the blankets of the service bed we kept in the office for the night duty officer.

"Tell them I've been asleep for hours. Tell them anything!" He panted. I quickly helped him off with his boots and tunic and tucked his blanket neatly around him. As far as I was concerned he could go to the glasshouse for the rest of his life. How could a grown man be so idiotic and so thoughtless as to do such a stupid thing. It was quite beyond me. For a sleeping man, he simply reeked of beer and when presently, the policeman and his assistant came galloping into the office, Les was snoring over realistically.

'Where is he?" the policeman demanded, "Where is Ferriday?" I hung grimly onto the phone not daring to look. "He is sleeping over there." and I motioned to the bed in the corner. With no ceremony they tore him out of the bed. Les, feigning sleepiness, did his best. They took him into the little cabin bar which adjoined the office and gave him a thorough third degree.

Les had apparently an infinite capacity for a beer. No matter how much he consumed he never seemed to be drunk, and he really had had a skinful. The two police officers nagged and quizzed him incessantly, but he did not slip, he was adamant. Yes, he had been to the pub but had left just as it got dark, and came back to the hotel as he was tired. At eleven o'clock that night when I left in the duty lorry with the Night Fighter control crew, the three men in the bar were still hard at it.

Unfortunately, the reserve policeman had waited in the shadows of the churchyard in case Les had carried out his threat. Somehow Les had got into the bell tower unobserved, and by using his boyhood know-how of bell ringing, had rigged up a delay which had given him a good start and somehow or other he was out of the churchyard before the first chimes had echoed across the fields.

How he managed, in his beery state, to run the distance to Hope Cove, I'll never know but this was not the end. The following day he was taken to Plymouth where he was well-known and given a severe working over by the area commander. The turmoil he had created in military circles took weeks to die down. Nevertheless he had succeeded in his wish to bring a bit of light to the dreary world and to ring the bells that Christmas 1941.

Chapter Six: Jack takes to the air

As an unofficial reward for my successful endeavours in reducing the annoying jitter on the Beaufighter radar picture tubes, I was doing my first stint of operational flying, as a radar observer, from Exeter. The week was almost up, and apart from practice interceptions I had as yet not even smelt an enemy aircraft. The week before had been a week of intense night activity for Bolt Head with the German pilots trying their luck in single-aircraft experimental nuisance air raids. This week, however, business had been very bad.

The operational information that had to be extracted by the radar observer from his equipment and fed to the pilot, was difficult enough under normal night-flying conditions. With the pictures, however, bouncing erratically at a fantastic speed, the interceptions set up by the GCI were being lost due to the indistinct pictures on the airborne radar. The Mark IV Aircraft Interception (AI) radar as installed in the Beaufighters had two cathode ray tubes with which the target bomber ahead of the aircraft could be exactly positioned with respect to the night fighter. One tube indicated whether the target was to the left or right of the fighter, the other tube indicated whether the target bomber was above or below the fighter. By careful observation of these two pictures, the radar operator could guide his pilot by giving a running commentary.

This was accomplished by presenting the signals received by the aerials on the left and right wings on one screen, and the signals received by the aerials situated above and below the wings on the other screen. To present all this information at a high speed, a small electric motor rotated a series of delicate aerial switching contacts. In this way a continuous picture was presented to the observer, who could make operational use of the four signals. The adjustment and servicing of these tiny phosphor bronze switch fingers was an art I had learned working on a CHL/CDU station which utilised the same principle for obtaining accurate bearings on ships.

On this my final night at Exeter airport before returning to Hope Cove, it was raining miserably. Frankly the prospect of my last night's flying in this shocking weather did not appeal to me in the least, yet I was determined not to miss the final opportunity before returning to the ground end of the interception organisation. It was most uncomfortable as in the few seconds taken to leave our transport and climb into the aircraft, a stream of cold rain had somehow or other got down the back of my neck. With a minimum of delay we got underway and trundled towards the end of the runway. The engines were run up, and we waited for quite a considerable time before permission was given to take off. Dimmed by the rain, the lights of the flarepath head raced by and we were lifted by the powerful radial engines into the moonless black night.

After flying through the cloud for some time, the rain stopped and the stars gradually appeared in the top of the Astro-Hatch [a transparent dome on top of the fuselage of the aircraft through which observations were made in night-flying navigation]. The stars gradually became brighter and brighter until one could almost see, even on a moonless night like this. The bright sheet of the Milky Way was a very useful backdrop for target visual identification. By the time we were ready to return to base, the whole fantastic array of stars would have rotated around on the axis of the Pole Star, which somehow or other seem to be mounted on the front part of the Plough. Up there in the night skies, the stars took on a completely different meaning and I regarded them as close friends helping to show us the way home.

When the engines had settled down to steady revs, I switched on the AI set, keeping the brightness low so that I could still retain some of my night vision. Under the control of Exminster GCI we had started the usual practice interceptions. I muffed the first interception, but quickly restored my honour a short time later. Once I had the feel of the equipment and the confidence of the Polish pilot, we intercepted our companion quite easily and followed him through a series of quite complicated jinks. Even with the improved split switch operation the AI trace was still showing the characteristic jitter but it was now easily usable down to the shortest normal range.

The maximum range of the radar on a target aircraft was slightly less than the height of the Beaufighter. To the pilot, the range to which he could be directed onto the target was most important, as with the impossible visibility at night, it was touch and go whether you could see another aircraft at all, even at a hundred feet. However, if one knew where to look, aircraft could be seen at about three hundred feet. With the AI working well, it was possible to direct the fighter pilot to within about 300 feet of the target. This was only made possible by the genius of Dr Blumlein of the EMI who developed the Blumlein modulator still used to this day.

It is interesting to note that the airborne radar, which had been developed almost completely at the time of the outbreak of war, suffered only from this minimum range deficiency. If the radar operator in the night fighter could not put his pilot near enough to the enemy target, it was quite obvious that the target would never be seen visually, and given the coup de grâce.

Dr Blumlein's contribution to the radar science was phenomenal. This brilliant scientist was also the inventor of the modern stereophonic record. His idea was patented in 1938 and of course, only came into production after the war, with the birth of the long-playing record. This scientist, who gave so much to the science of radar, was killed in mid 1942 in a West Country air crash when completing his tests on the fantastic bombing aid anti-submarine weapon, known as H2S. Many of the thousand and one electronic inventions incorporated in this radar were tribute to his genius.

As the night progressed, we "played" over the English Channel each taking turns at being fighter and target. The rules of the game allowed the target pilot to choose his height, but this always had to be between 10,000 and 15,000 feet. In the early hours of the morning we had finished what was perhaps our last practice interception in the centre of the Channel, when we were informed by the controller that there were things afoot. We were directed onto an incoming aircraft flying above us at a comparatively slow speed. A secret agreement with our own bombers necessitated their return to Great Britain after a raid at a height of 10,000 feet or less. Any aircraft flying above "angels ten", was almost definitely hostile. Not however, until an aircraft had been positively identified visually as a hostile could the cannon and machine guns of the Beaufighter be brought to bear.

A series of vectors brought us up behind the invading aircraft just before we crossed the coast somewhere near Portland. We finally established our own radar contact with the raider at a maximum range. He was high and to our starboard. The GCI had given us the correct speed and we slowly approached towards the rear of the aircraft. We climbed slightly, the picture was healthy and far better than that of the Beaufighter. As the range decreased I began to get very excited. The tubes indicated that the enemy aircraft was half a mile ahead and up to our right. I decided to leave the tube to take a look outside in case the raider took evasive action. If he jinked, by watching the tubes, it was more than likely that we could stay on his tail. We drew closer and closer to the target until it disappeared into our transmitter pulse. The pilot informed me that he could see nothing. With his permission I climbed and raised myself up near the astrohatch and looked forward out of the small aperture. Just as I reached this position I was astonished to see some large circular coloured neon lights pass over and narrowly miss our starboard wing before getting lost in space behind us. Our pilot could now see the aircraft and he closed in and tried to identify it. Quite suddenly we could both see the chunky outline of a Wellington Bomber [i.e a friendly British fighter] and once again the rear gunner had opened fire on us. We dropped down and to the left, while our pilot told the GCI their fortune in no uncertain terms!

The tracer from the machine gun floating by had looked so pretty and harmless, fortunately the machine gunner had scored no hits. This was the frustrating end to my short tour and our time was now up. It was past three in the morning when we turned west and flew overland towards Exeter. As we nosed down into the black cloud, the moon was just rising. Inside the cloud it became completely dark once again and detuning the radar receiver, I picked up the radar beacon at Exeter and gave my pilot the gradually reducing ranges to Exeter airport.

As we began to come out of the clouds the rain started once again and began to pound us fiercely, as we started to let down. The radar beacon allowed us to make a comfortable approach and I breathed a sigh of relief when the aircraft banked slightly and the lights of the flare-path came into view. There were some vicious gusts of wind cutting across our path. Then with a series of mechanical jerks, the pilot lined the aircraft up on the runway.

I braced myself as the aircraft touched down with a series of rather heavy thuds. The aircraft then rolled smoothly along the strip and that was that. We were safely home. With these thoughts in mind, I relaxed. Quite suddenly I found myself pushed sideways and upwards against the equipment with something sharp digging deeply into the middle of my back. What on earth had happened? We seemed to be turning very violently and I could not move as I was kept wedged against the bulkhead of the aircraft.

The smooth run of the wheels was now replaced by an extremely heavy vibration and for a moment I could not make out what had occurred. The pressure had now abated and I braced myself for whatever was going to come next. After what seemed a long run, the aircraft trundled to a halt. We turned and taxied towards the tarmac.

"Not to worry", said the pilot. "We only skidded right off the runway". He sounded quite nonchalant, but my heart and I'm sure his, was still beating violently. I was now more than satisfied at the prospect of going back to the more mundane and less hazardous duties at RAF station, Hope Cove.

My father respected the Polish pilots very much. He writes admiringly of their exploits, their bravery and their determination to defeat the enemy.

303 Polish Squadron, which had fought magnificently during the Battle of Britain, had now divided its experienced pilots and formed a number of sister squadrons. One of these was number 317 which was moved to Bolthead to carry out the new offensive against the western coast of France.

Equipped with the most modern type of Spitfire, and led by a squadron leader with a phenomenal flying record, this mixed bag of experienced pilots and young keen beginners, prepared for the initial experiments. During the detailed briefing for the pilots I explained the need for the low approach to avoid possible radar pick up. It was decided that three sections of Spitfires, that is six aircraft, would sweep along the coast in a search for radar stations and carry out a general reconnaissance. I gave the airmen detailed instructions in the use of the IFF [Identify Friend or Foe] set and pointed out the procedure in the event of an emergency. They were to avoid flying wing-tip to wing-tip and to keep below 500 feet for the whole of the overseas trip and for the last twenty miles or so they would come down to 0 feet with their propellers practically skimming the wave tops. They were to conserve their petrol, record the period of duration of any excessive demand on their fuel supply so that on their return to England we could make a careful check on their petrol consumption and replan any further operations on the basis of this experiment. No use was to be made whatsoever of the VHF radio telephone during the trip across the Channel and all local flying was disallowed until our friends had reached the coast of France. This was to give the German radio snoopers no advance warning of the 'rhubarb' [small-scale low level fighter attack in search of targets of opportunity.]

Early one morning when Bolthead was still shrouded in a grey mist, the six aircraft took off and vanished instantly from our sight. For a short time we followed them on the radar tubes of GCI Hope Cove but due to their low altitude we soon lost radar contact with them. With our equipment, however, we kept watch on the sky through which the Poles would have to fly.

If any of the pilots had experienced engine

trouble, his use of the IFF, 'Mayday', switch would have allowed us to direct a Walrus Air-Sea Rescue flying boat to his immediate vicinity. This way it was possible for him to indicate his distress on the radar screen and the radio telephone would not be used, thereby alerting the watchful German defenders.

Watching the coloured sector clock in the operations room, we allowed the periods of time to elapse for the fighters to make land-fall in France. A further 20 minutes for the actual 'rhubarb' and then all concentrated on the two radar tubes as we anxiously awaited the first 'blip' of an aircraft or the powerful transmission of an emergency IFF signal. About a quarter of an hour after they should have turned for home, we heard a babble of indistinct radio telephone conversation which the VHF direction finding station reported as coming from our lads.

A short time after the signals, a clear call came from the leader informing us that they were now starting for home. This news shocked us all, as having extended their visit to France by another 15 minutes, they could in theory, no longer reach the English coast. We could do nothing but literally bite our fingernails and wait to see the aircraft one at a time go down into the sea.

The flying discipline of the Poles was very good and they did not use the radio telephone but when they were half-way across the

Channel we picked them up on our radar. We gave them a call to see how they were faring and the leader was quite happy with the position. We asked for their fuel state and he evaded a clear answer and said they had sufficient fuel to get to base. In a short time they appeared over Bolthead and after one port orbit they one at a time dropped over the hedge and landed in front of the GCI. A fuel check revealed that despite their extended operation, they still had a considerable quantity of fuel in their tanks. It seems that these Polish airmen knew far more about the Spitfire than did even the technical instruction books!

For some months the squadron carried out a continuous series of attacks on the French coast. The art of returning to base with a mere smell of petrol vapour in the tanks became a point of honour amongst these excellent airmen. They were a queer mixture of gaiety, passion, skill and nonchalance. That they wielded more than considerable power over the opposite sex was evident by the increasing stream of distraught parents making enquiries about their daughters at our orderly room! Their skillful flying and contempt for danger had to be seen to be believed.

I was busy one day in the operations room vehicle when the service policeman at a small guardroom telephoned and reported that two obstreperous Poles had entered the confines of the GCI perimeter despite his energetic protests. These airmen were not allowed any detailed knowledge of the GCI station in case they crashed in enemy territory and were captured. It was, therefore, official policy to keep them away from the small compound. I descended the steps at the rear of the Crossley lorry and passed out of the light trap, shielding my eyes from the unaccustomed glare of the sun. I could see these two men hard at work with a long tape measure measuring the distance between the rotating aerial trailer and the front of the operations room vehicle. I ordered the two pilots out of the compound and as they had finished taking their measurements they promptly departed without any further trouble. I returned to my job of preparing copy tracings for 10 Group, of the previous night's fighter operations and forgot about the incident.

As I was concentrating on my work I paid little attention to the sound of aircraft engines which I vaguely heard in the distance, until the operations room vehicle was suddenly and frighteningly shaken by a vicious roar of engine and blast. Dropping my drawing paraphernalia I moved towards the ladder at the rear of the vehicle to nip down quickly and see what had transpired. Before I could reach the door of the operations room the whole vehicle was shaken by a second blast. Tumbling down the stairs I ran outside to see what was going on. High overhead two

Spitfires were doing Victory Rolls and our service policeman was shouting his head off in fright.

The two Poles had been measuring the gap between the two vehicles to see if a Spitfire could possibly fly between them. The fact that a thick copper, 200 lbs gauge feeder cable was stretched between the operations room and the aerial trailer and was just 15 feet (4.57m) above the ground, did not in any way deter the airmen. They had flown their Spitfires under the feeder cable and between the two trailers. It seems the 24 inches (61cm) was, in their opinion, sufficient clearance for the wingtips of a Spitfire! The fact that they might have crashed, killing both themselves and everybody in the operations room, besides wrecking the GCI did not even enter their heads!

On the following pages: Letter Jack sent to Dally (Dell) in January 1942. The incident with the discipline is interesting for as the senior NCO Jack was responsible for discipline at the station.

Cottage Hotel,
Hope Cove,
Nr Kingsbridge,
S Devon.

My Dear Dally,

For the first time since I came back I am beginning to see daylight through the pile of work. I even managed to stage a trip to Exeter yesterday.

At least I got so far as a RAF station Exminster where I stopped for a chat. Exminster is about twelve miles from Exeter. When I was chatting to a pal of mine by the name of Denny Stone, a breathless WAAF ~~dashed in with the news~~ that at Group Captain and A V Marshal had landed at Bolthead.

These were the gentlemen I missed when on leave and I should have been there to see them. To cut a long story short, we managed to get back to Bolthead, that is 45 miles in about 65 minutes which necessited much hurry and did we go!

Still everything went off alright; I was not made to suffer for my indiscretions. The rotten part is that I was going to Exeter to prepare for the twenty seventh of the month.

146

It seems that I might be rather late now but better late than never. (I hope you dont mind). I'm enclosing a picture of Hope Cove Hotel (ARROW) and the worst part of the sea front. I'll send some more beautiful pictures that will really shake you.

It's one of the most beautiful places imaginable and I'm not kidding.

Dont laugh now but I've got a most awkward job. I've got to put a chap on a technical charge for failing to salute a commissioned officer because his wife was hanging on his right arm. A return of the sentence has got to be submitted because the charge is being preferred by the Special Security Police. Still, I'll see that he gets off alright. Supposing somebody had reported a senior N.C.O pushing a pram full of coal up Ealing High Street, I wouldn't know where to look.

Still nobody has so why worry. I'm sorry Dolly but this is my last sheet of this paper so I'll finish now until tomorrow night.

Until then, I remain,

yours for ever,

Love,
Jack

X   X   X Fri
X   X   X Sat
X   X   X Sun

147

Chapter Seven: Operation Rutter

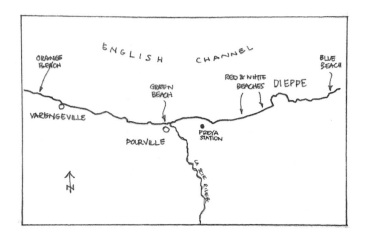

Map of the objectives in the Dieppe Raid, which took place on 19 August 1942. The German Freya Radar station was situated on the top of the cliffs between Pourville and Dieppe. This was the station that Jack was asked to investigate.

Jack writes:

I had some time previously volunteered to Squadron Leader Keir at 78 Wing Headquarters at Ashburton [Devon] for dangerous operations, and had received a special army training to defend and maintain myself in action. After some four years of working on each and every facet of the radar science, I was in the unique position of being able to examine radar equipment and accurately estimate its purpose, and perhaps, its modus operandi. I would also be able to assess with a reasonable degree of certainty, when confronted with the radar equipment, which were the parts worth removing and taking back to England for further examination.

The first intimation I had of an impending operation was when I was asked to report to Air Ministry in London. After an interview with the senior intelligence officer at Air Ministry I was asked to agree to conditions of non-capture, [if it was decided to send me to enemy occupied Europe].

Air Vice Marshall Victor Tait [Director of Radio in 1941, the Director of RDF, the early name for Radar in 1942] was most unhappy at the execution clause in the arrangements, and I gained the impression that he had disapproved of the whole idea. During our discussions I feel that he did his best to make me withdraw, certainly giving me time to think it over. Being Jewish, I could expect no quarter from the SS if captured. Ten Canadians of the South Saskatchewan Regiment were to be delegated to assist me in any operations I wanted to carry out, and as a sort of negative safeguard they were to make sure that I did not fall into enemy hands alive. I myself agreed not ever to be captured.

in one Li.i.i.

(ii) Prisoners will be left in possession of all badges, identity discs, decorations, etc.

758. Enemy Weapons and Equipment

Enemy weapons and equipment are required in large quantities for intelligence and training purposes. All ranks will collect all possible enemy weapons, equipment, and articles of uniform, which will be taken to the Administrative Dump, vicinity 231682. The officer-in-charge of the dump will arrange for its embarkation.

(d) Interrogation.

(i) All interrogation will be confined to information of *immediate* tactical value and identifications (which will be reported without delay to Force H.Q. Ship No. 2 (H.M.S. " Fernie ").

(ii) Interrogation officers will accompany the forward troops landing on " Green " and " Blue " beaches (Camerons of C. and R. Regt. C.).

759. Search of Buildings

Field Security personnel will be detailed to search buildings and H.Q.s under the supervision of the O.C., Field Security Section. Plans and Instructions are part of this Appendix.

760.   **SEARCH OF " JUBILEE "—PERSONNEL AND TASKS**

Serial.	Detachment.	Personnel.	Tasks.	Remarks.
(a)	(b)	(c)	(d)	(e)
1	Intelligence ..	4	(i) Capt. T. H. Insinger will establish P.W. Cage in the vicinity of " White " beach, assisted by Capt. E. D. Magnus. (ii) Lieut. I. T. Burr is attached to Camerons of C. (iii) Lt. F. Morgan is attached to R. Regt. C.	—
2	Detachment of Provost Coy.	3	R.V. 0600 hours at Tobacco Factory with Capt. Insinger or Capt. Magnus to man P.W. Cage.	—
3	F.S. Section ..	14	Search of buildings and H.Q.s under supervision of O.C., F.S. Section.	—
4	M.O.I. ..	9	Search Town Hall and carry out special mission.	Travel on L.C.T. 13. Under command of Capt. P. J. Harratt. H.Q. to be established in vicinity of Dental School—with seven assistants from 3 Cdn. Lt. A.A. Regt., R.C.A.
5	10 Inter-Allied Commando.	7	(i) Selecting limited number (up to 12) of French nationals for evacuation. (ii) Liaison with French population. (iii) Distribute propaganda pamphlets and aux. posters.	Travel on L.C.T. 14. H.Q. to be in vicinity of schools on Rue Desceliers.
6	R.D.F. expert	1	Examine and search R.D.F. Station, Caude-Côte, with assistance of one Field Security O.R., as detailed.	Travels with S. Sask. R. on " Prince Beatrix." S. Sask. R. to provide adequate protection as R.D.F. expert must under no circumstances fall into enemy hands.
7	M.E.W. ..	1	Search town for material required by his department.	Travels with Prov. M.E.W. in L.C.T. Group 7. Can use P.W. Cage as H.Q.
8	S.I.O.	2	Special mission.	Travel on L.C.T. 11. Four assistants from 8 Cdn. Recce. Regt. (14H). .

761.   **INSTRUCTIONS FOR SEARCH PARTIES**

Pourville, Caude-Côte.	1 R.D.F. expert. 1 F.S.P. 1 M.O.I.		Beatrix. Beatrix. Beatrix.	Att. to :— S. Sask. R.	R.V.—On Eastern end of beach where sea wall bends (and river enters sea through pipe).	
Serial.	Objectives in order of priority.	Location.	Route.	Estimated time of starting search.	Material required.	Remarks.
1	La Maison Blanche	Pourville. (exact location unknown — off of white house).	—	Soon as possible.	Officers' papers.	Officers' Mess.
2	R.D.F. Sta. ..	Caude-Côte. 208683	As situation demands.	—	Details and parts of R.D.F. apparatus.	R.D.F. personnel must be given sufficient protection to prevent his falling into enemy hands. (F.S.P. and S.O.E. to assist R.D.F. expert)

Note.—R.D.F. Station should ...d.fied as soon after capture as possible. On conclusion, party will proceed to P.W. Cage via 6 Bde. H.Q.

This is a summary of the 'battle orders' for the Dieppe Raid, which include 'special' instructions for the RDF (Radar) expert who was to be given 'sufficient protection to prevent his falling into enemy hands.'

My father underplays this in *The Wizard War* but in later life he spoke of this interview with bitterness. There was no question that he was being asked to go on a suicidal mission. The odds of his coming back were very slim. What made the whole decision more difficult was the conversation he heard as he left the room. Referring to an Army Captain who is quoted in *Green Beach*, as he reached the door, he heard him remark grumpily to his colleagues "you would think they could find someone better than a Jew for a special job, wouldn't you, what ever it is?"

That evening he went to the cinema with his fiancée Dally and his mother. The inner turmoil for him was painful. His mind was occupied with the conflict; he was being asked to give up his life for his country, but his country (or some of it) still considered him to be a second-class citizen and interloper. Understandably pre-occupied, he walked out of the cinema as the credits finished at the beginning of the film. He did not say goodbye. My mother and grandmother looked up and he had gone. They could not begin to know the thoughts that were passing through his mind, but often referred to his disappearance as one of his secretive "quirks".

In February 1942 a group of commandos had attacked the Wurzburg radar installation at Bruneval, northern France and taken parts of the installation and instruction manuals back to Britain, giving the British a good understanding of its capabilities. Unlike the Freya radar, the Wurzburg had a limited range of 70 km [43 miles] and was used primarily for gun laying to shell ships sailing off the coast.

In the aftermath of the raid the Germans realised that their radar stations were vulnerable and over the ensuing months the defences around these installations were greatly increased.

The RDF bulletin a top-secret fortnightly news sheet was sent under secret cover from the 60 group to Jack he writes in *Winning the Radar War*:

In addition, because I had been involved in radar developments from the beginning I had easy access to the scientists with whom I had previously worked: Watson Watt, Preist, Blumlein and others. I therefore had an up-to-date knowledge of our own development and made my contribution to them Flying Officer Thomas Hunt was the person to whom I nominally reported at that time, and it was from him that I first learned about the magnetron, which was undoubtedly the most important invention in the entire radar story.

For the first time a single piece of metal was a complete radar transmitter. The cavity magnetron's hitherto impossible short wavelength of one 10th of a metre compared to what both the Germans and we had so far achieved; this was nothing short of miraculous. The shortest wavelength on which either side operated up to that time was half a metre; the wavelength of the CHL system was 1.5 m, that of the Freya 2.5 m, and the CH of course worked on a very long wavelength of 12 m.

The war-winning cavity magnetron valve devised in 1940 by Professor J T Randall and Dr H A H Boot. Its unique ability to transmit microwaves at very high power enabled radar equipment to be built that was infinitely more powerful and accurate than anything previously designed. It was Jack's knowledge of this valve and the radar equipment, that made it imperative that he was not allowed to fall into enemy hands alive.

Ted Bell, whom we know and who worked in Radar straight after the war, wrote in June 2020:

> The Cavity Magnetron Oscillator is a device which generates High Frequency Microwaves. It is basically a metal ring with a number of precision holes (cavities) around it forming the Anode and a central Cathode. When the electron stream attempts to pass from cathode to anode a powerful magnet diverts the electrons so that they continue to circle between cathode and anode. As they pass each precision cavity it will resonate to produce microwaves, in much the same way that a flute produces sound waves when air is blown across a hole. These can then be channelled by a waveguide to a radar transmitter to produce a powerful high frequency pulse.

In 1941 the magnetron was seen as a rugged, reliable innovation, capable of mass production and more powerful than was possible with conventional thermionic valve technology.

The cavity magnetron was not a new idea. The radar developed with the cavity magnetron used microwaves and was able to detect objects as small as the tip of a periscope of a submerged U-Boat submarine in all weathers and even in the dark. This made it possible to attack these submarines even when they were not on the surface.

Stuart Leasor, the son of author of *Green Beach*, James Leasor wrote in May 2020:

When my father, James Leasor, was writing the story of Jack Nissen's epic Dieppe Raid mission, which was published as *Green Beach*, Jack came to stay a number of times at my parent's home in Wiltshire. I remember, during a family supper in what must have been the school holidays, Jack saying that he was going to show us something that helped win the war, and he produced this small cylindrical metal object with some holes drilled in it from his pocket. He then told us how it revolutionised the accuracy of radar. It was seemingly just a routine supper to a teenage boy and yet it was one of those fascinating evenings that you remember for the rest of your life.

Jack's knowledge of the latest developments in radar technology, especially the advantages of the cavity magnetron, together with his detailed understanding of how the whole radar defence organisation worked, could under no circumstances be allowed to fall into enemy hands. That is why his superiors deemed it necessary to have him accompanied by a bodyguard with orders to ensure that he would not be captured alive.

During the process of my army training some six hundred miles to the north, in Scotland, and after signalling my delay, I had arrived back at Bolt Head a day or so late. The newly arrived general duties officer now in charge of the

155

administration staff of the aerodrome took a dim view of my comings and goings. I was, however, not allowed to tell him or anybody else about my special trip. This particular officer had gone to the extreme of having an entry made on my RAF record sheet. Without his knowledge, and on a very high level, this entry was immediately nullified. The fact remains that I could tell nobody at all on my station just what I was up to. It meant taking leave and organising with Air Ministry for short term posting to Air Ministry units in different places to cover my men. During one of these short-term postings to Air Ministry Unit Long Cross near Egham, just outside London, I spent an enjoyable few days with Bill Cox who had just earned his Military Medal at Bruneval [a previous raid on a German radar station]. On going to London for Operation Rutter, I had to consider that my posting might this time be permanent and perhaps, if I were unlucky, sealed with a bullet. [The Bruneval raid 27-28 February 1942, codenamed Operation Biting, was a raid on a German Wurzburg Radar Station at Bruneval, northern France by members of a parachute regiment aimed at 'stealing' as much of the radar equipment as they could carry back to the ships. The success of this raid alerted the Germans to the vulnerability of their radar stations and they carried out major defences to all their installations].

For some time a Scots radar specialist had been

picking up the threads of my job, and I could now leave permanently if necessary.

The transport was waiting outside, and in no time I was on my way. Some hours later I arrived at Richmond Terrace, Whitehall, Mountbatten's secret headquarters of Combined Operations Command. After finishing a short briefing, I paid a brief visit to the senior intelligence officer at the Air Ministry, King Charles Street. In the company of a pleasant army security officer, I travelled by way of the Southern Railway out to the Port of Havant, a few miles from Portsmouth. Together we caught the ferry to Cowes, the beautiful yachting centre on the Isle of Wight, and I had my first meeting with the wonderful Canadians of the South Saskatchewan Regiment.

Having dutifully handed me over to the commander of the SSR's Colonel CCI my escort returned to London. [Charles Cecil Ingersoll Merrit was awarded the VC for his gallantry during the Dieppe Raid]. With Sergeant Black's able assistance I settled in for the night. The Canadians were billeted in the magnificent seaside mansion of Osborne House on the outskirts of Cowes [Isle of Wight]. This castle-like building had been a Royal holiday resort in the not too distant past [It was Queen Victoria and Prince Albert's residence]. The high-ceilinged rooms with panelled walls were now the temporary lodgings of the Canadian farmer soldiers. They showed the utmost respect for Osborne House and its surroundings. When they departed, it was left in the same spotless condition as they had found it. Early on the following morning I heard the walls echo to the voice of Sergeant Major Stromm. Without a doubt he was Canada's secret weapon. I remember thinking that, more than likely, sergeant majors in different uniforms of bygone ages had also made their voices echo off those ancient ramparts.

The Isle of Wight had been the scene of most of my pre-war vacations. Usually my holidays had consisted of camping and cycling in the beautiful English countryside. The strong legs I inherited from my cycling days were, in the near future, to decide whether or not I stayed alive.

Over the years my personal history was to be bound to the beautiful Isle of Wight. Immediately after the war I returned for my honeymoon to Shanklin, just three miles from Ventnor.

A day or so after my arrival at Cowes we embarked on the Princess Beatrix, a beautiful Dutch motor vessel of very modern design. Its low superstructure made it a poor reflecting surface for the German radar at Pourville, under whose watchful but rather myopic eye we were a few hours later to be disembarked. Whilst awaiting sailing instructions the ship lay offshore at anchor. We did not sail that night as the weather reports were bad, and without air support the operation could not proceed.

We stayed on board the ship and sampled naval rations so wonderfully different from our landlubber food. On the following day Commodore Lord Louis Mountbatten, the chief of Combined Operations came aboard and had a word with each of the specialists. Being an ex-signals officer himself who had initiated many of the naval theoretical textbooks on radio, I discovered that radar was an open book to him. The troops were assembled on deck and the CCO [Commander Combined Operations] addressed them. He warned the Canadians to expect the worst, and to use their training to the best of their ability in the forthcoming battle. The address was short and sweet and to the point. After three rousing cheers, he made for the next ship in the convoy. Sadly, the weather deteriorated and we spent yet another three exasperating days aboard the Beatrix waiting for an improvement in the weather.

By now the Canadians were getting despondent. Their main fear was that the operation would be called off. They were most anxious to get into action and had many conversations where it became apparent to me that as long as they managed to take one of the enemy with them, they had no real concern about the probabilities or possibilities of coming back.

The Luftwaffe now became interested in our fleet dispersed over the Southampton Water. After a late evening reconnaissance we received an early morning visitation by four JU88s. At six o'clock in the morning these aircraft swept in low to avoid being picked up by the CH station at Ventnor. I discovered afterwards that they were however, plotted by CHL Bembridge and after having dropped their bombs they had been traced back to France by two sections of Spitfires. The damage however had been done. [JU88 Junker 88, a German multi-role plane of which 15,183 were built].

Two troop carrying ships loaded with landing craft, the Princess Astrid and the Princess Charlotte had been hit, with no casualties, however. Strangely enough, the bombs pierced the ships, and exploded in the water below, causing no heavy casualties. On board the ships were the Royal Regiment of Canada. After the attack one of the ships was found to be taking water badly so troops were disembarked and Operation Rutter was cancelled.

On the morning following my return to my radar unit in South Devon we received an early call from four Focke Wulf 190 fighters. Though they approached over the wave tops they had been detected in reasonable time and two fighters had been scrambled from our own airstrip. These Focke Wulf pilots had been radar briefed. By approaching low along the Salcombe estuary, and then turning and climbing over our headland on which our fighter strip and GCI were situated, they approached the runway with a minimum of warning and suddenly appeared over the GCI.

Without doubt the heavy camouflage saved this station. Each F/W dropped a large bomb in the vicinity of the runways.

They then proceeded to fly over the air strips and machine-gun the hedges, presumably searching for the GCI which for some time had caused the Luftwaffe much heartache. The GCI controller visually observed the German attack, and calmly spoke to the patrolling Typhoon fighters, giving them a running commentary. He did not rotate the birdcage aerial of the GCI as this would have immediately called attention to the station and would most certainly have attracted a devastating attack. The nearest bomb dropped less than a hundred yards of the GCI, which was situated beside the east/west runway.

As the first Focke Wulf turned for home, out to sea, a Typhoon claimed the luckless pilot as he passed over the rocks at the end of the runway. The other Focke Wulf seemed not to have observed the attack and proceeded with a fiery destruction darting to all the odd corners of the headland obviously searching for the GCI. When they eventually pointed their nose south to return to France, the two Typhoons attacked them. The miniature air battle, low over the sea occurred in full view of excited GCI crew. The Typhoons then chased the FW all the way back to France and a further FW was reported shot down as it climbed over the French cliffs.

After a hectic night's operation in which GCI Exminster and Hope Cove had cooperated successfully in the shooting down of some bombers making for the Bristol area, I came off duty about seven o'clock in the morning, very much the worse for wear. I spent some time in the Nissen hut I used as an orderly room, completing some paperwork before returning to the hotel for some sleep. My orderly room telephone rang, and the guard reported that a Humber Snipe was waiting at the guardroom for me. The driver and companion had no Air Ministry experimental station permits and, quite correctly, the guard had refused to allow them into the station. He asked if I would come across and check the credentials of the visitors. It transpired that the car had been sent to take me post-haste to London.

Forgetting my tiredness, I made the driver follow me through the winding Devon lanes to my hotel at Hope Cove. As we approached the sea, I signalled for my friends to slow down. We climbed over the brow of the last hill and stopped for a second or two and surveyed the beautiful scenery. The hotel below, the sandy coves and the sweep of the sandy beaches bordering the green sea with a backdrop of crystal blue sky. I took in the breathtakingly beautiful scene and hoped that this would not be my last opportunity to take in the wonderful Devon vista. Regretfully, I started off again and, in low gear, I descended the dangerously steep drive and parked near the well - timbered front door of the hotel. I walked across the lounge to the office; finding no messages I ordered some tea for my chauffeur and his companion. Excusing myself, I plodded wearily upstairs and made my way along the passage to my blue suite.

Opening the door, I once again thought, will this be the last opportunity to make use of my pleasant room with its excellently appointed and luxurious facilities? I ran the bath, stripped and stepped down into the sunken blue bowl and relaxed completely. Well, even if I didn't come back, I had more than enjoyed my long stay in this wonderful place. I thought back to those early days of hardship when I first arrived in South Devon. Hope Cove station was now well-developed and highly successful operationally. It was now the centre of a whole defence complex.

Chapter Eight: Operation Jubilee

My father at twenty-two was going to go on the most dangerous of missions. He knew the implications, but was still keen to start. His importance was underscored by the fact that a car picked him up from Devon, took him to Whitehall in London and then again he was escorted down to Southampton.

We slowly climbed the steep drive out of the hotel and got on the road to the cathedral city of Exeter, the first town through which we would have to pass. It was a long run to London but my driver wasted no time. Fatigued after the long night's operations, I fell fast asleep and only awoke hours later as we entered the western approaches to London.

Our first stop was at Air Ministry, Whitehall. On arrival there I reported to the Senior Intelligence Officer, who suggested that there was still time for me to back out of the operation as the no capture clause still held good. I pointed out that ten men of the SSR [South Saskatchewan Regiment] had been detailed to ensure that I complied with these instructions. I picked up the small bag enclosing my varied assortment of tools which included a compact electronic test meter, a collapsible hacksaw, side cutters, pliers and various other devices intended to assist in the speedy dismantling of enemy radar. With this bag over my shoulder I left Air Ministry for the headquarters of Combined Operations at Richmond Terrace, Whitehall, just a few yards away.

Here, I was officially informed that the Dieppe Raid was once again on, under the new name of Operation Jubilee. Transport was provided for me and an hour later we arrived in Crondall [Hampshire]. In an elegant Victorian mansion, a large number of excited officers were readying themselves for their parts in the resuscitated operation. After a snack, I had a short chat with a Marine Major and then I was driven at high speed to Southampton where we entered the King George V Dock. It was now about 8 pm. Alert naval sentries were everywhere, obviously primed for trouble.

In the beautiful summer's late twilight I boarded the *Invicta* to a chorus of good-natured cries.

Many years later after he wrote this, the Imperial War Museum invited Jack to give an oral history of his war years. In 1989 Jack described how moved he was at the stupendous welcome he received. The memory was as fresh as if it was yesterday. I have transcribed some of it below.

"So with a marine major escort and a SOE chap we drove to King George V docks in Southampton, and as we got to the dock gates I heard this terrible racket going on in the distance. I said "What's all the noise" and the SOE chap said "it's those crazy Canadians kicking up a row".

"As we drove along in this big smart car towards the side of the ship, it was the *Invicta*, I could see that all the soldiers were hanging over the side of the ship bashing on the side with their tin hats and kicking up a row booing and jeering as they saw the car approaching the gangplank, and on the side of the ship they had in chalk "Get us action or get us home." They were on the point of mutiny and had had enough. They either wanted to see some fighting or go back to Canada. It was very touching. [moving]

"We came down to the foot of the gangplank.

"As I opened the door the booing was terrible and I thought they thought it was another officer to give them some more small talk.

"And as I stepped down I had a white face because I lived at night and they knew me. The boys knew me, the boys of the South Saskatchewan Regiment and they were the ones who were kicking up the row.

"They looked down and when they saw my white face they realised if it was me coming and not some other officer, then there was definitely going to be some action.

"They went dead quiet and all of a sudden there was an incredible cheer. They were so thrilled and excited that this thing was really going to happen. I shall never forget that as long as I live."

The whole ship had been waiting for me. The gangplank was lifted and the ship was on its way. We passed the chequered forts in the centre of Southampton Water and gradually

the shore receded. In the remote distance, the
sirens of an air raid alert sounded. Hastily the
crew got to work and rigged up a dummy
canvas funnel and in the mellow evening of
midsummer, we set out on our one-day
excursion to France. The Canadians were
jubilant. The fact that thousands of troops had
known for a whole month the location of the
raid did not dampen anybody's spirits. The
possible complete lack of security worried
nobody. At long last we are going to have a
crack at the Nazis. Morale was very high as the
troops busied themselves preparing the new
issue of arms and equipment, priming them
ready for action.

Leaning over the handrail and hypnotised by
the phosphorescent wake, I had time for quiet
thought. I realised that things were more than
likely going to be quite difficult, but I was
thrilled and exulted at this prospect, of at long
last seeing some action. To the strains of the
Canadian marching tune at the time 'Praise the
Lord and Pass the Ammunition' the men
prepared themselves for battle. Standing on the
deck and listening to the buffeting of the canvas
dummy funnel, I remember thinking, thank
God at last we are going to give them something
back.

I paid a visit to a Lieutenant Colonel Merrit the
CO of the SSRs who, just a few hours later, was
to earn the coveted Victoria Cross. His huge
frame was reclining on and spilling over a tiny
bunk. This handsome young officer was the

picture of good health and happiness at the thought of the action ahead. I checked with him that my execution squad was intact and we discussed trivialities for an hour or so. Though a hectic day was ahead of us, neither could sleep.

At about 2 a.m. the ship's loudspeakers announced that we should slightly inflate our combined operation-type navy blue Mae Wests worn under our battledress, as we were now about to cross the German minefields. The *Invicta* proceeded at high speed, its bow wave, so one of the sailors cheerfully informed me, helping to deflect any of the mines that might still be around. Our ship was leading as my party of SSRs were to land first and assault the radar station in the half-light. Other SSRs were to secure the bridgehead ready for the later landing of the Canadian Camerons, who were to leapfrog ahead to an aerodrome a mile or two inland.

Some twelve miles out from the shore our engines faltered and stopped. The assault landing craft were lowered and using rope nets over the ship's side, we disembarked according to plan. Amid muted happy cries that echoed off back from our mother ship, the landing craft powered by the two V8 engines started the long journey to France at a speed of six knots: Next stop Green Beach, Pourville. [Each beach where the troops were to make shore was given a colour; blue, red, white, green and orange].

Twelve miles was just beyond our tested range

of German radar. Here we were, a line of ships, some ten miles long, lying just twelve miles off the coast of a heavily defended continent, disgorging more than four thousand fighting men in seven long columns. It was a beautiful night, but of course with no moon. The most easterly column of landing craft were No 3 Commando. They were some seven miles east of our column. The most westerly line of craft carried No 4 Commando under Lord Lovat. We were running neck and neck with these landing craft of 4 Commando who were a mile or so to our right. The two commanders had the task of spiking the radar - directed heavy guns mounted to the east and some to the west of Dieppe so arranged to dispose of any ships that might lie off Dieppe in a possible invasion attempt. More or less dead centre of the operation were the tank landing craft, which were to land some thirty tanks on the main Dieppe beach. After accomplishing their objectives in the Dieppe town these tanks were to fan out to the suburbs, some to the east and some to the west. Those moving to the west were to appear inland from Pourville where our men were to rendezvous.

After completing our operation we were to be carried by the tanks back to Dieppe town, where we were to be evacuated from the dock area.

Our landing was timed to occur at first light. Taking advantage of the poor light, we were to storm up the hill, and to be amongst the

German radar station defenders with rifle and bayonet before they could man their pill boxes and machine gun posts. As we would have to assault the station with its barbed wire defences after this initial attack we expected a stiff fight. Our chances, however, were excellent providing the navy dropped us at the appointed spot with the necessary ten minutes cover of semidarkness. This was at a point on the Pourville beach where the river Scie flowed into the English Channel. When we landed on the banks of this river, we would have a steady unimpeded run of a mile or so to the perimeter wire of the radar station. We surmised that the slope would be well defended, but the semi-darkness and surprise were to be our main weapons. The lads of the SSR had every reason to be supremely confident.

The trip from the mother craft to the shore was to last about two hours. The assault landing craft travelled at a speed of about six knots and had some twelve miles to cover. The sea was choppy, salt spray splashing over the ramp of the landing craft. Our thoughts were all of eager anticipation of the coming fight. Though there was no moon, looking back from my position on the ramp of the assault landing craft I could see a sea of helmets right back to the rear of the craft where on a miniature bridge a young naval officer and seaman steered the vessel.

The quiet purring of the two V8 engines was a most reassuring sound. In true navy style this system of telegraph bell signals to the engine operator kept the assault landing craft on its right course. The first hour of the trip seemed interminable. When the first half of the journey was completed and we were still some six miles from the coast, a brilliant flare to our east shot into the sky lighting up the surrounding seascape.

It lit up the long lines of landing craft that stretched far into the darkness that was streaming into Festung Europa [Fortress Europe]. After being in complete darkness, the glare of the flare as it drifted down into the sea was painful to the eyes. Our landing, which needed complete surprise to stand a chance of success, now seemed to be revealed to the whole of the German Wehrmacht.

Immediately heavy fire broke out in the vicinity of the flare, tracers flashing this way and that. A vicious but confined naval battle ensued. After about ten minutes the tracers subsided. "Now what?" we all thought. We had no idea as to what had happened, or of the outcome of the battle. Complete radio silence prevailed as our landing craft continued on its way to Pourville. There was an eerie quiet as the men contemplated their fate. German E boats escorting a small convoy, which sadly had been plotted by CHL Beachy Head had just practically massacred the whole of No 3 Commando.

A naval rating queried the Canadians in a loud voice, "Do we turn back?"

Barney's [a tough SSR member of Jack's bodyguard] thick Irish sounded loud and clear.

"If they try to turn back, we take over this craft and go in ourselves."

He was not joking; that was the spirit of the men. They had been idle too long and wanted action at any cost. Their attitude as expressed only too often was "We don't mind dying as long as we take one of the enemy with us!"

Some ten minutes before landing, an army canteen of rum was passed around. I took my share, though even without the rum, I was highly exhilarated at the prospect ahead. Quite suddenly and without warning, there loomed overhead the massive black cliffs on the top of which, though shrouded in darkness, would be our radar station. With a massive clanging of engine-room bells, which echoed up and down across the cliff face and beaches, our landing craft engines went into reverse bringing the craft to a halt. Turned to starboard we steered west parallel to the beach and towards Pourville village. Surely it seemed the whole German army must have heard our echoing bells? We could expect a hot reception from the natives.

This is the point at which our part of the operation became doomed. For a while the ALC [Assault Landing Craft] steered west and then turned 90° to port, increased the speed of its engines and started to run onto the beach. We prepared our weapons and braced ourselves for the landing shock. With a horrible grinding sound, we beached, our ramp dropped and we sprang ashore. At long last we were on enemy territory. To the thunder of dozens of pairs of army boots we sprinted up the stony beach. Instead of open land before us, we found a high sea wall engulfed with masses of barbed wire ad odd notices ominously inscribed "Minen". On the other side of the barbed wire was the sea wall and behind that the double-storey villas of the beach front, at Pourville.

Chapter Nine: Under enemy fire

We had been dropped nearly 400 yards too far to the west. With great gusto the Canadians laid down their bangalores [torpedoes used by combat engineers to clear obstacles] and set to work with wire cutters and scaling ladders. More by luck than judgement, a gap was found in the wire and, my execution squad following, I jumped over the seawall in front of the villas. An alarm shrilled out on the first floor just over my head, followed by an ear- splitting female scream. What respectable young lady would like to wake up at the crack of dawn and find a mob of soldiers storming her residence in the half dark?

A heavy machine gun opened fire on us from the direction of the hillside. Huge expanding orange tracer balls floated towards us and whipped over our heads. This gunner caused a few casualties in the last of the SSR landing craft to beach. We now had to penetrate Pourville, turn left, move out to the east and then start the long run up to the radar station. Already other pill boxes and machine gun posts on the slope up to the station were manned. A stream of fire, punctuated now by the heavy crump of mortar shells, caused our first casualties.

At this point I lost the first of my assistants. Despite the long range, the gun fire was quite accurate. It was now light enough for the German machine guns to operate without tracers and, in the face of intense fire from the machine guns directly in front of us, we moved towards the radar station. After leaving the town we had to cross a small bridge over the River Scie.

Beyond the bridge, the Dieppe road took a right incline inland. We made our way forward with bullets thudding into the turf. For the machine guns on the hill, the whole area was laid out like a map beneath them. Skilfully camouflaged, the machine guns were causing lots of casualties amongst the advancing Canadians. The bridge behind us now seemed almost covered with bodies, some still moving. Certain posts [gun emplacements] caused considerable delay, but Colonel Merrit himself had pitched in to take a particularly difficult strong point, helping once again to get the men on the move. Even a small bump in the ground seemed a haven from the rain of bullets.

Many of the bullets seemed to be from rifles situated almost behind us but it was not possible to see the snipers. The machine guns kept us crawling and dodging into odd spots of cover, the mortar shells then flushed us out. From the machine gun posts, prisoners were taken, who with their pink-and-white faces looked very much like high-spirited schoolboys. The schoolboys' comrades however, had by now made a layer of bodies almost two deep across the bridge. They were terrified and expected to be killed. Under some form of escort they were chased back to Pourville and had to run the intense gauntlet of their own friends' fire.

The whole of the hill slope up to the clifftop where the radar station lay had been cleared of foliage and shrubbery in preparation for an attack such as we had launched. There was no doubt that proceeding in this direction up the hill there was no chance of anyone reaching the radar station alive. Accurate artillery support fire to deal with the heavy machine gun posts was our urgent requirement. A few small Smith [anti-artillery] guns would have made all the difference. We urgently needed artillery support but there was none, and even the 3-inch mortars which were of limited range, had run out of shells.

For some time I sat in a hedgerow which bordered the road on the inland side of the station. I watched the pitifully small force of Canadians, many of them wounded, gradually come to realise that this was as far as they were likely to get. With persistent accuracy the alert German gunners fired down on us over the barbed wire of the station. The barbed wire which was supposedly going to be breached by bangalores was itself quite beyond our reach. At this point-blank range it was suicidal to show your body for even a second.

After a long stalemate, I made my way back to Pourville where BHQ [Brigade Headquarters] had been set up in the village. By now my whole party of assistants had disappeared, either dead or wounded. At BHQ I made a meal of some brown bread, biscuits and tomatoes supplied by some local French girls. I sat on my tin hat in an alley beside the building and devoured this food, together with some rather sour wine. The girls, aged about 16, pleaded with us to take them back to England. In my best schoolboy French, I pointed out that this was quite impossible. I handed them the special thin pamphlets printed in French, which advised them to keep away from us and avoid German reprisals.

Overhead British aircraft streamed inland, seemingly unopposed.

The Dieppe Raid Combined Operations battle was controlled from 11 Group Operations Room at Uxbridge. The Battle of Britain had started just two years before and the scene at Uxbridge was very much the same except that the table now showed plaques concentrated around Dieppe and not Dover.

Flights of British aircraft flew in impeccable formation inland and as yet there seemed very little reaction from the German Airforce. In fact, it was almost nine o'clock before the Luftwaffe at Dieppe appeared in reasonable strength.

It gave us poor foot-sloggers a wonderful feeling to see the masses of Spitfires flying in perfect formation, from England daring the German fighters to come into action. Odd German aircraft were attacked by the Spitfires as they appeared. These combats always ended in a spiral of smoke, and usually with a delicate white disc of a parachute slowly descending.

By about 9 o'clock, the noise of the German machine guns and artillery, as well as the roar of the multitude of low-flying aircraft now in combat with a newly arrived Luftwaffe, made it hard to hear oneself speak. The temporary deafness and rushing noise that followed a shell burst in one's vicinity were almost a relief from the intense racket. Despite the cheering effect of the masses of friendly fighters, we seemed to be unable to get the support we needed in order to breach the defences on the hill immediately in front of the radar station.

A forward observation officer, equipped with radio, who was supposed to spot for naval bombardment, seemed to be unable to obtain any assistance from his seaborne artillery. His job was complicated by the fact that it was extremely difficult to see from where the enemy fire actually came.

During our training exercises it had been quite easy to pick out snipers even at that long range, by the flashes of their guns and the smoke of their rifles. Under combat conditions these helpful effects were completely absent; even when we were under intense fire, the enemy weapons could often not be spotted. Despite super-human efforts by Lieutenant Colonel Merrit, it became obvious that nobody would ever reach the radar station alive. This was the conclusion I came to after another hair-raising trip back to the front. Without a miracle, we could never get near the station which lay high in front of us in full view. I think it was Murray

Austen, sheltering in a hedgerow after a particularly vicious burst of machine-gun fire, who smilingly said to me, "There is your radar station." I am afraid my answer was most uncomplimentary, and certainly not printable.

Four hours had passed since our landing, and we were getting nowhere. Our troops had been horribly mutilated, and it seemed to me that another plan was required if we were going to get into the radar station. I have mentioned before that military planning included the arrival of Churchill tanks from the direction of Dieppe. These were to approach the Pourville region from behind the headland which we were investigating and to sweep inland and arrive a mile or so from where we were being held. I decided to initiate a plan to enlist the help of the tanks. I told a junior officer at BHQ what I intended to do, and asked him to organise some volunteers.

We formed a party from some of the SSRs and Camerons, and made our way inland. Keeping to the road, we climbed the long hill out of the village. Even at this extreme range the snipers were scoring near misses amongst my companions. As we drew level with a large double-storey house on our right, which I think was La Maison Blanche, German shells blasted the building. Artillery fire, presumably aimed at our party by the German gunners was rather high and the shell had overshot, causing some spectacular destruction. The trees on either side of the road gave us some form of cover. Quite suddenly, in front of us and just across the road a group of German soldiers appeared and peppered our small group with light machine guns. We all carried rifles at the port and as one we fired at these luckless soldiers, who fell immediately. We had no casualties. I went over to collect shoulder tabs or any other intelligence information from the fallen soldiers. One had fallen backwards through a hedge, another lay beside him parallel to the road on his back with his arms outstretched and one knee bent as if he were resting his young, white dead face and looked terribly pathetic. What a crazy game this war was. This lad's masters, however, were still wiping out huge sections of Europe's population and pity at that time could not be spared. As the German soldiers had no worthwhile documents, we proceeded inland.

After a short time we turned left through a small forest in which we found a large stone tower. We stopped for a while and whilst we were under cover a single mortar shell dropped within a short distance of our party. At this point I noticed that new field telephone wires of the Don 8 type always seemed to run parallel to our path. Even across the clearing and in the direction we intended to go was a pair of these telephone wires. I detailed two soldiers to sever these wires whenever we located a new pair. At points where these wires had been stapled to the trees and telegraph poles, the staples were invariably shiny, and it was quite obvious that they had only quite recently been placed in position. It seemed that these communications had just been installed as part of a carefully thought-out defensive plan.

We left the clearing and prepared to go down the hill inland to the east. Quite suddenly an aircraft flying at treetop height appeared overhead with guns blazing. As we dropped to the ground I noted the square at wingtips of a Messerschmidt 109, or so I thought. This aircraft, however, had the black and white stripes of one of our own support aircraft. Nevertheless it narrowly missed wiping out most of our party. This was the first Mustang plane I had seen, and it nearly scared the life out of me and my helpers.

As we descended the exposed part of the hill, bullets began to thud into the turf at our feet and one of the men was immediately hit in the shoulder. We stopped in a ditch under a copse of trees to apply field dressing. Removing some Horlicks tablets from my escape set, I issued them to my tired assistants.

With a short audible warning a mortar shell landed amongst us. It was quite obvious that even this remote area had been accurately marked as part of a defensive scheme and that somebody, with the aid of the telephone wires, presumably was spotting for the mortars.

We moved forward onto the open face of the hill and into the accurate long-range machine-gun fire. We took turns running the gauntlet up the hill over a sharply projecting piece of ground. The sound of heavy bullets thudding into the other side of the small hillock was most unhealthy, to say the least. We came up behind a smallholding, and passed through an orchard with bullets zipping amongst the apples, to which we thankfully helped ourselves. We then came to a road running in a north - south direction. Here was a sight I had been praying for, telegraph poles, heavily laden with a multitude of wires and going in the general direction of the radar station. Detailing two Canadians to assist me, I tried unsuccessfully to bring the pole down. Climbing the pole, I cut every wire within reach.

Beside a house which lay some way back from the east side of the road was a Peugeot car which seemed at the time to be quite a find. Possibly, we hoped, it would assist in us making a speedy rendezvous with our tanks. Whilst fiddling with the car in an effort to make it start, a small dark young French man with a moustache came running from the house. He told us in high-speed French and sign language to leave the car alone. A burly Canadian said menacingly in his own brand of French hand over the keys or else… The Frenchman insisted that he did not understand and in any case he did not have the keys. As he refused to cooperate we tore the spark plug leads from the car rendering it temporarily non-operational. We felt he must be some type of collaborator and had no qualms in immobilising his car.

Proceeding along this peaceful country road the

horror of the fighting seemed incredibly remote. Coming over a rise as we rounded a corner, we came almost face-to-face with a group of German soldiers. They were as surprised as we were. Taking cover we opposed each other. From up the lane there came a series of German shouts - presumably their companions were being called to come to their aid. By now it must have been almost 10 o'clock, and as yet we had seen no evidence of our tanks or troops from Dieppe proper.

We had no wireless communication and did not know that the tanks we so confidently expected lay completely smashed to smithereens on the promenade of the main Dieppe beach. Not one had managed to get beyond the town.

After a hurried discussion, we decided it was useless to engage what was obviously a superior enemy force. Making cover for each other, and under heavy fire from our German assailants, we proceeded back by the way we had come. Had we known that General von Runstedt [a German Field Marshal] had some time previously told the 11th Panzer [tank] division to clean up the breakthrough at Pourville, we would not have been so tardy in making our decision to retreat. By 1 o'clock that day, this powerful armoured fighting force was within three miles of our incursion. Even retreat proved difficult; at times they had us trapped in culverts and ditches, but eventually, after we had made a solid stand and inflicted casualties on our German opponents, they decided to break off the action.

Proceeding shoreward, we came to the country crossroads which I had originally reached from the beach. Though most of the Canadians seem to have retired, the remnants were still held by the heavy machine gun fire on the west side of their radar station. I noticed that the steady fire over the last few hours had almost denuded the lush hedges. Looking up the hill to the station, it seemed so near, and yet out of our reach. The CHL-like aerial was now locked with its vertically polarised dipoles looking straight out to sea.

An order had apparently been received to "vanquish", that is to leave the beach head at 11 o'clock. Instead of from Dieppe town we were now to leave from our own beach, Green Beach, at Pourville. As we reached the village, snipers in the houses were once again causing casualties.

Feeling rather depressed at our reception we returned to be BHQ on the beach front. I spoke to Colonel Merrit, who was quite naturally feeling extremely upset at the loss of so many of his fine young lads. His face was white, black rings of strain under his eyes. "Look what they have done to my boys," he said. "They have torn them to pieces." Amongst those waiting on the beach there had been a first-class massacre. Despite his intense exertions, and obvious signs of fatigue, he still retained his command. Many of the SSRs had long since waded out to sea and scrambled aboard landing craft offshore, and were already heading home.

Looking out to sea from the beaches there were the burnt out remnants of at least half a dozen landing craft which had tried to beach. They had been hit by German artillery and left derelict.

Smoke obscured what was happening out to sea where some naval craft were moving around. Pourville itself, is a small village in a cleft between the cliffs with rising ground to the left and right.

On the right headland looking out to sea was the radar station from which a barrage of intense artillery and harmless long-range machine-gun fire still poured. From another small cleft in the cliff to our left a murderous fire rained down on the front of our small BHQ building. The German troops had also began to filter into Pourville village, and were attacking from inland with small arms. Mortar and artillery shells were gradually reducing our BHQ building, which lay on a corner. To the front, a window looked out to sea. The entrance to this corner building was on the road which led up the hill and out of Pourville. The Germans who had positioned themselves in the houses surrounding, kept up a steady fire, were of no great menace, but the heavy fire from the cleft in the cliff to our left was causing steady casualties. Each taking his turn, we tried first with a Bren [light machine] gun and then with an anti-tank rifle to put this machine-gun post out of action. We merely succeeded in increasing our casualties, and field dressings seem to have run out.

When we had all but given up trying to eradicate our opponents in the cleft, a small naval craft equipped with a multitude of anti aircraft weapons approached the German heavy machine gun post from the sea. In a shattering concentrated broadside they put it out of action.

After a session on the guns I retired to a narrow passage between the buildings to rest my aching and bruised shoulder. From this vantage point and looking east in the direction of the radar station I could survey the whole scene. The British fighters were still sailing majestically from the sea. Four serenely flying Spitfires stepped up, with a leader high in front, cruised almost over our heads and the tail end Charlie [last aircraft in the formation] lower than his friends, and weaving quickly from left to the right.

"It's a shame we can't tell them what a pickle we are in," said one of the Canadians. "I suppose we are here for the duration," said another.

With mortar shells landing continuously on our little BHQ and with machine-gun and small arm bullets raining on us from various directions, for many of us the duration was likely to be terminated quite promptly.

"If only we could contact one of the planes," said a Canadian jokingly.

I replied, "Why don't you try to signal one of the Spits with a mirror?"

To my delight the Canadian brought out a mirror and I'm quite sure he thought I might be able to signal to a Spitfire with it.

Despite their bravado these chaps were quite worried.

"Have you seen any radio packs around?" I asked.

One of the lads informed me that there was a damaged unit in the yard behind the building. When I went into the back yard, I was surprised to see a number of young French girls still there. They were pathetically waiting for our evacuation and hoping to go with us back to England. After trying to explain our serious predicament, in no uncertain terms I once again handed out the leaflets. Despite the fantastic fire raining down on the building from all directions they refused to depart. They could not, and would not, believe that we ourselves had no longer any method of getting back to England.

I inspected the radio set that had been badly damaged, mainly in the battery supply unit. I asked around if anybody had seen another set somewhere near the post. Possibly by cannibalising, I might have been able to make one set work long enough to report our position. One young soldier told me of a set which lay in the middle of the road, still on the back of its unfortunate owner, some distance up the hill.

The prospect of going back up the hill and under the general fire from the newly arrived Germans was not very enticing. However, with two soldiers I started out. Surprisingly enough, we made considerable progress by keeping to the limited cover on our side of the road.

Without being fired on, we eventually reached the radio set, still on its original owner's lifeless back. Once we had crawled level with the radio we were presented with the problem of going out into the middle of the road, exposing ourselves in order to retrieve it. The spot seemed comparatively peaceful and one of the Canadians crawled to the lifeless signalman. He experienced considerable difficulty in removing the set, whilst lying prone. As he sat up to get to grips with the problem, we heard shouts from down the road and thudding of boots. Bullets started to kick up the dust around our friend in the middle of the road, who had now managed to remove the pack set. We gave him intense covering fire as he galloped back to the ditch with bullets spitting at his heels. He fell into the ditch dragging our prize.

We reached a small crossroads and had to decide how to get across without catching the eye of our opponents. The Germans were still firing at our original position some twenty-five yards away.

Using the harness I strapped the pack set firmly to my back and clattering my rifle at the high port, I rose and sprinted madly across the road into the ditch on the other side, nearly crowning myself on a culvert. My companions then followed me, but under fire from the Germans, who had now noticed that we were getting away. One of the chaps had his battledress slashed, but was not wounded. We now had a long clear ditch down into better cover, but decided to wait until our opponents showed their hand as the road curved and our backs would be exposed to the general fire if we carried on our way.

The German soldiers followed us keeping to cover on the other side of the road. Finding a suitable spot we set ourselves up to engage the German soldiers. Whilst we were waiting for them to arrive, a sharp crack followed by a short scream from one of my companions was the first intimation that somebody was firing at us from behind. I felt a terrific smash on the head accompanied by a blinding flash in my left eye. I flattened myself behind a small mound as another crack followed by a violent tug at my pack set indicated that I was the next target. I blazed away with the whole magazine from my Lee Enfield [a magazine-fed rifle] and then moved off like a crazy crocodile further up the ditch to a point from which I had cover from the house. The shots from the rear sounded as if they were fired not from a service rifle, but a light calibre sports gun. My head now ached shockingly, and I had to close my left eye which hurt severely. Feeling dazed, I realised that I now had only one assistant. To make matters worse, some other Germans were now moving up the hill keeping to the hedge opposite presumably to see what the noise was about.

We slid and scrambled down the ditch until we entered the more heavily built-up section of Pourville, where we came under heavy fire from the other German soldiers, safely hidden in the houses on the other side of the road.

Reaching a street intersection, we found it was impossible to cross the road without exposing ourselves to the point-blank suicidal fire from the concealed enemy. We stayed at this juncture for some time wondering how to negotiate the crossing before the soldiers realised that they could attack us with impunity from the way we had come. We were stuck, and desperately searched for respite from the continuous fire from the Germans opposite. The steady thud of bullets into the soil, a few inches from our faces was more than a trifle disconcerting. To make matters worse, we had all but run out of ammunition.

Quite suddenly we noticed a squat little Frenchman wearing a flat cap and a chest full of First World War medal ribbons, walking steadily and purposefully up the road as if he were on a Sunday stroll, completely ignoring the shouts, warnings and whistling bullets directly between us and the Germans. The enemy held their fire, and we quickly grasped the old man's intention, [The Germans had strict orders not to kill French civilians] darted smartly across the road and scrambled behind a low wall which gave us more than ample cover.

Thanks to this brave old soldier we were able to continue on our way down to BHQ.

Chapter Ten: Escape and rescue

We eventually arrived back at BHQ [Beach Headquarters] very much the worse for wear but with our prize seemingly intact.

I was both worried and puzzled about my head pains as I could no longer have sighted my rifle. I was quite sure I had not been hit. Once among friends in the little backyard of our BHQ, I removed my helmet to douse my head with some cold water, and the pain abruptly ceased. The near miss on my helmet had rammed the headband hard into my left temple, and must have constricted the blood flow or depressed a nerve on my head. Needless to say, I was immensely relieved when the pain stopped. At least I would be able to use my rifle. I now hung onto my Lee Enfield like a drowning man to a straw.

With my temperature somewhat down, I felt more like looking at the radio set. From a French girl, I received some more food, and sat down on the granite slab with the set before me. I had long since lost my little bag of tools and when my companion retrieved the other radio, using a bayonet as a screwdriver, I set to work. When I had partly dissected the radio a mortar shell landed on the roof and showered both me and my equipment with brick dust. I moved my paraphernalia under a makeshift shed and inspected my apparatus. With a vicious air battle going on overhead, our building under mortar and machine-gun fire, conditions were not exactly suitable for fixing radios. I thought at the time how wonderful it would be to put the sets up on my bench in Tottenham Court Road, and sit down quietly, and get on with it. It did not strike me that I might not ever see Tottenham Court Road or even England again.

After careful examination of the two sets I realised that I was wasting my time. The batteries in the new set were also ruined. My companion, as well as a group of onlookers, were all heartily disappointed at the news. My work was terminated by another fall of masonry on the shed accompanied by the arrival of a wounded Canadian NCO, who told us to get our guns and get on the job as our inhospitable hosts were now arriving in larger numbers. As I went out of the east door the Canadian beside me took a bullet which slashed his forearm and tunic. With another Canuck [Canadian] I fought the man, distraught with pain and shock, took him back indoors and helped to apply some field dressings.

Once again I went to the front of the building and took up the prone position and let off some steam with the Bren gun at the Germans in the west cliff who had now come back into action after the temporary incapacitation by the Royal Navy. Though I burnt my hands quite badly on the barrel I somehow did not feel the pain. The skin went brown and hard. My face was sore and smarting from the constant gravel blast from near shell bursts. After wasting our time, energy and friends and achieving nothing with the radio, there was something particularly positive and satisfying about the Bren gun. At least I was firing directly at the enemy. The young Canadian who handled the loading of my Bren pans had been enjoying himself immensely despite the heavy ominous thud of the bullets, from the heavy machine gun we were opposing. He was singing over and over again one verse of the Canadian marching some "Praise the Lord and pass the ammunition and we'll all stay free." Though I held the Bren gun well into my right shoulder, it was once again feeling quite sore.

My personal position was now indeed dire. My promise still stood: Capture now seemed inevitable and rather than be captured I was contracted to be killed or intended to commit suicide, and capture now seemed completely inevitable. The German troops could be seen as they darted across the road coming down the hill, and taking up positions in houses on both sides of the road. In English, a German soldier shouted something like, "Come on Jock, stop fighting. That's enough." At that stage there seemed to be very little future in the struggle. For some time now the German Air Force had been fully engaged with the RAF overhead. On that day, I am sure I saw every type of German aircraft in the book. At any time one could watch a dogfight and see one or two parachutes coming down.

The RAF lost twice as many aircraft in the fighting

over Dieppe than on any other day, even during the Battle of Britain. In nine hectic hours the RAF lost about one hundred aircraft. The German aircraft losses were just over fifty. It must be remembered that losses are always harder when operating over enemy territory, especially when assaulting ground targets.

The German losses too equalled their worst day of the Battle of Britain, 15 August 1940.

The fight was now on in real earnest. A Spitfire screamed seaward, a white cloud of glycols streaming behind it. It flew up to where the pilot from a low altitude took to his parachute. A small naval vessel made a beeline for the airman. At one stage I felt sure I had seen a four engine German "Condor" [originally designed as a peacetime airliner] dropping bombs on our ships. To use aircraft of this size in the battle area, crowded with Spitfires and Mustangs, showed in my opinion that the Luftwaffe really scraped the bottom of the aircraft barrel.

A vic [flying in 'V' formation] of three JU88s, came low over the sea from the direction of Dieppe. One was streaming glycol but still maintained excellent class formation. At a low altitude they turned together and flew back towards the smoke and attacked the landing craft concealed thereunder. They then turned to the east and disappeared still flying at zero feet.

This kind of intelligence information was just what we required. That is just what was available to the Luftwaffe for the defence of northern France. After the Dieppe Raid, the German ground and air defence was increased enormously. This was of course one of the objects of the planners. Winston Churchill promised Stalin that some form of major distraction would be imposed on the Germans. Stalin, whose Russian armies were being hard-pressed, had been most insistent and Churchill's word was his bond. After Dieppe, the Germans poured enormous numbers of man hours, material and personnel so urgently needed for the war in the east into an enormously improved western defence system. This build up continued for the next two years and during this period of time, the intense German defensive effort helped to divide the German war effort.

I sat on my helmet in our corner room by the sea and mentally reviewed the situation. Bullets ricocheted across the window as I tried to decide what to do next. It must have been almost midday, and I had precious little time in which to decide anything. Outside, under smoke supplied by another naval vessel, a newly arrived landing craft was seen to be cruising up and down parallel to the shore about eight hundred yards out to sea. Every time its ramp appeared out of the smoke, a shell or two would burst in the water nearby making enormous fountains of water. Intense fire continued to rain on our little HQ from all directions. If I was to get away, it would have to be now or never. I did not intend to be captured but suicide seemed a negative way out. Most of the men around me were incapacitated in one way or another. I approached one or two of the men who could still run, and asked whether they were prepared to take a chance on running the long gauntlet of fire to the sea, despite the fact it would have been easier and safer for them to remain behind and be taken prisoner. Roy Hawkins, [Roy Hawkins and Jack met again after the war] a field security sergeant, decided that he would go with me, and in a short time he had about a dozen men. A collection of smoke canisters was organised which could be thrown across the promenade road by the non-runners. This would give us some temporary cover from very heavy fire of the watching Germans.

The machine guns in the west cliff had now been reinforced by some other heavy machine gun and the hail of lead from the west was unbelievably intense.

I firmly tied two primed grenades to my webbing belt, one on my left and the other on my right. If hit and wounded on the run, I intended to detonate one or both of these grenades. It would have been all over very quickly. From my escape set in my right trouser leg I swallowed a large white pep pill and waited until the assault landing craft was cruising in our direction.

On the word 'go!' we made smoke, dashed over the promenade, jumped clean over the wire, and narrowly missed landing on the bodies of the killed and wounded lying unseen to us in the shadow of the high seawall some ten feet below. I had almost landed on top of a young red-haired soldier who lay rolled and strapped in a casualty stretcher. He, and many others were waiting for the evacuation of the wounded, which now would never come. He seemed quite unperturbed, and smiled engagingly at me. He made some kind of crack, which above the racket I did not hear. Having landed nearly on top of him I ruffled his hair as an apology and carried on. Under the cover of the wall where I'd hoped to run there was a seemingly endless line of bodies strewn over the stones. In the jump, one of my hand grenades had come adrift. Picking it up, I held the other tightly and ran as near to the seawall as the bodies permitted. By the shouts from above it was apparent that the Germans had noted our getaway, and were coming down to the seawall to finish us off as we dashed along the beach. Some of my party were already hit and I was expecting the impact of a bullet any second.

After miraculously running at least one hundred and fifty yards east towards a breakwater, I turned out to sea and ran down the beach. At this point others of my companions were hit. Running into the sea with bullets spitting at my ankles, the small arms fire reached a crescendo. In no time we were almost waist deep and I shouted to the men around me "Swim underwater, as if you are hit." We swam a considerable distance beneath the water, which was luxuriously refreshing, and when we surfaced, the firing was no longer so severe.

We swam towards the smoke and the general direction of the landing craft. Shells, presumably aimed at the LCA [known as Landing Craft Assault] sent up an enormous amount of water that completely blotted out the sun. Though the bursts were some distance ahead the blast from the water was numbing. When I was completely and utterly exhausted, the half open ramp of the LCA suddenly loomed over my head and two strong arms reached out and helped me to scramble aboard. I felt an intense feeling of relief as I lay exhausted and breathless in the warm water swirling around the deck of the waterlogged landing craft. My troubles were over, or so I thought.

My father often told me that although exhausted and gasping for air he managed to blurt out "Pick up my friend?" A Cockney voice of the sailor answered, "What do you think this is, mate? A number eight[6]?" They picked up Roy Hawkins and they were on their way back.

Maybe, with the benefit of hindsight, it was probably just as well Jack and his 'bodyguard' were unable to get into the radar station at Pourville. The Germans may have been lulled into a false sense of security, knowing that the British had been unable to capture any of the top-secret radar equipment in their

---

[6] The number eight bus went out to Forest Gate in East London.

station.

What the Germans did not realise was that a radar expert had been able to inspect the aerial array at close quarters, and from his knowledge of British radar could determine from the actual configuration and size of the individual elements in the aerial array, and the fact that it could be rotated, the wavelength on which it operated and how advanced it was. The disruption of the telephone system in the whole of the area around Dieppe had been one of the main objectives of the allied forces, and because the telephone lines to the station had been severed they had to resort to their radios. The information that Jack was able to convey to R V Jones and Victor Tait when he returned to England, together with the analysis of the radio transmissions from the Freya radar station, enabled the boffins to create Mandrel[7], the radar jamming device that was to prove so valuable on D-Day, some two years later.

Mandrel jammers were used by several squadrons to protect the advancing Allied invasion force from German radar detection. A reinforced squadron used mandrel to screen 1000 transport aircraft carrying airborne troops for the landings east of Caen and on the Cherbourg Peninsula, and the seaborne invading forces.

---

[7] Mandrel was a radar jamming device developed by the scientists and technicians working at TRE Malvern, using the information gleaned from the German radio transmissions and Jack's observations of the German Freya radar station.

Chapter Eleven: Jack returns to Blighty

We cruised a while longer, looking unsuccessfully for further survivors. Roy Hawkins and I were apparently the only two of the group to get aboard the landing craft. A pain in my side turned out to be the lone grenade on which I was lying. I decided to hang on to that weapon just in case I might still need it. After a luckless search for swimmers, the young petty officer guided the LCA seawards and out of the smoke.

Instantly, we were attacked by two German fighter aircraft at sea level - it seemed that the whole German Wehrmacht was conspiring in an effort to prevent my getaway. As one fighter started its attack on the LCA it was made to turn 90 degrees to port and then 90 degrees starboard in a crude effort at evading some action. Though effective on one aircraft, the other nearly always made hits, which kicked up an infernal din on the armour - plated side of the landing craft.

The petty officer ducked down, lifted a Lewis gun and holding it to his shoulder sprayed the attacking aircraft with bullets to the accompaniment of some choice epithets which I am sure were much more damaging than worthy .303 bullets.

We made for a barge, which seem to have every ack-ack weapon in creation on its armoured deck. As we gradually approached, its fire persuaded the attacking fighters to desist. We drew alongside and to Cockney cries of encouragement from the marine crew of the flakship [a heavily - armed ship to protect other sea vessels] we were helped aboard. I found an open spot and lay on the warm armoured deck looking up at the air battle raging overhead.

A parachute billowed out from a Spitfire that had been shot down. The crew cheered the marine OC [officer commanding] as the barge turn slowly and made towards the falling parachute. We were pipped at the post by a small destroyer-like ship which went after the pilot like a greyhound. It received some hearty good-natured boos from the gunner crew who badly wanted to rescue one of our pilots.

The long, wide flat barge had a high bridge arrangement at the station on which stood the fire control officer and his underlings. The deck seemed to me to be covered with every conceivable anti - aircraft type weapon that had ever been made, and most of the time they all seemed to be in operation. To the accompaniment of a series of excited warning shots a JU88 flying at fairly low altitude was seen to be making a rather slow bombing run on us from our stern.

To fire at this aircraft the gunners had to fire directly over their marine OC's bridge. The staff on the bridge all ducked, and this seemed to cause the gunners much amusement. The first bombs dropped very short and as the JU 88 continued over the barge a black explosive ball was placed just in front of its fuselage and another inside it. The accuracy of the gunners was uncanny. As the bomber swept overhead, they all followed with their guns. They seemed to score many hits, but with no apparent effect. Quite suddenly and unexpectedly, from the side of the ship a JU88 appeared at a low altitude and very close. It dropped a bomb which seemed to send a pillar of water up to the heavens, and lifted the barge perceptibly, dumping it back into the sea. The gunners were all waiting for it as it passed to the other side of the barge and a cheer went up as the aircraft crept away low over the sea leaving a long trail of smoke.

Many German aircraft were now around and the gunners were in continuous action. A Royal Marine crew member gave me a dry battledress with the Royal Marine insignia, and a large tin of corned beef which I ate ravenously. The barge had now turned for home, travelling at a ridiculously low speed and with German aircraft constantly making passes. We were making rear cover for a destroyer-like ship, which was some distance ahead of us. Its speed was far greater than ours and in no time we were almost alone on the sea.

Below the steel deck was another deck some seven feet down. I went below, and the horror and stench of the wounded that greeted me, made me quickly return to the upper deck and fresh air. I had not realised that all these people were on board. The racket below when the guns were fired defies all description, and in any case it was far more interesting on the deck. Some naval people were working on the wounded and seemed to be doing a fantastic job. The moans and groans and stench were far too much for my stomach.

Travelling slowly across the Channel after our belated departure we reached Newhaven at midnight. After an exchange of light signals and much to our annoyance (some men had already died) the harbourmaster ordered us to stay outside the harbour. We were eventually allowed in at two o'clock in the morning.

By now the position below deck was awful, and to me it was the most horrible part of the whole operation. Wounds and death in action were one thing; they were all almost surgically clean, but to see and hear men suffer apparently unnecessarily with indescribable wounds was quite another thing.

As we approached the dockside, it was still a hive of activity under the screened floodlights. I could not find a private telephone, so with Roy Hawkins I located a spot in a warehouse where we dropped to the ground and slept like two dead men.

In *Winning the Radar War* Jack continues:

...... only to be roused a bit later by some Military Police poking us in the ribs. Roy spoke up for me, because as the lone man with an English accent among the Canadians, I was suspected of being a spy who had infiltrated and come across with the returning troops. It was some time before the Canadian interrogation officers accepted the fact that I was British and not a spy.

At about 5 o'clock in the morning, together with a group of Canadians, we were driven off to their headquarters in Sussex for interrogation. Realising the panic at Whitehall, I first of all put a call through reporting myself still alive and uncaptured. During the session I tried to bring home to the Canadian officers concerned that in my opinion the area had been thoroughly prepared for our attack. The fact that newly installed field telephone cables more or less covered the whole area over which we had to move had indicated that much intelligent German defensive foresight had been skilfully applied with devastating results.

I pointed out that the staples holding the wires onto the trees and poles were new, indicating recent installation. With the accurate German mortar shelling and its excellent coordination with its machine gun fire, the attackers, without some form of artillery, had had no chance of success.

The ultimate irony was that I could not tell of my mission. There would have been no point in telling these men that I had carried out a successful intelligence raid on a radar station – my companions had never heard of radar.

Jack and Roy Hawkins were finally debriefed by Capt. P Lieven who had his report written up and typed on 22nd August 1942. A second report by Lieut. H MacMillan was added to the debriefing notes. Both are included here.

The War Diaries of the Canadian Regiments involved in the raid on Dieppe include comments about Jack dated the day after the raid.

The whole document is reproduced below but I have transcribed the first paragraph as it is much easier to read.

Comments by SGT HAWKINS (11 F.S. SEC) and FLIGHT/SGT NISSENTHALL R.A.F. HOPE COVE (RDF EXPERT)

F/S NISSENTHALL had the task of obtaining equipment and information from the enemy RDF Station which – it has been intended to capture. For this purpose he was accompanied by Sgt HAWKINS. They crossed with with the S Sask R and effected what they claimed was an undetected landing at 0445 hours on GREEN BEACH. Fire was not opened on them until 25 minutes after they landed, when they were fired on by a MG from a building. The building was attacked and the MG was destroyed with hand grenades. General action was then opened. Both NCOs believe that the comparatively long delay in detection was due to the fact that a flight of Spitfires at the time drew the enemy's attention away from movements on the ground. Once action on the ground had begun, it became very heavy. Sgt HAWKINS and F/S

NISSENTHALL brought out several interesting points relating to enemy defences and tactics.

Interviewed by Capt P. Lieven G.S.O.3(I).

22 August 42

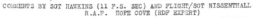

COMMENTS BY SGT HAWKINS (11 F.S. SEC) AND FLIGHT/SGT NISSENTHALL
R.A.F. HOPE COVE (RDF EXPERT)

F/S NISSENTHALL had the task of obtaining equipment and information from
the enemy RDF Station which - it had been intended to capture. For this
purpose he was accompanied by Sgt HAWKINS. They crossed with the S Sask
R and effected what they claimed was an undetected landing at 0445 hrs
on GREEN BEACH. Fire was not opened on them until 25 minutes after they
landed, when they were fired on by a MG from a building. The building
was attacked and the MG was destroyed with hand grenades. General action
was then opened. Both NCOs believe that the comparatively long delay in
detection was due to the fact that a flight of Spitfires at the time drew
the enemy's attention away from movements on the ground. Once action on
the ground had begun, it became very heavy. Sgt HAWKINS and F/S
NISSENTHALL brought out several interesting points relating to enemy
defences and tactics:-

USE OF MORTARS AND MG BY THE ENEMY

1. Both NCOs commented on the extreme accuracy of mortar fire; it was
possible for the enemy in many instances to score direct hits with
their first round. The NCOs attribute this to the fact that the
Germans in that area used extremely detailed and accurately worked-out
range cards. It appears that almost every point likely to be used by
an invader had been carefully taped from every mortar position.

2. The NCOs remarked on the perfect co-ordination between mortars and
MG fire as applied by the enemy. MGs were used extensively for
"herding" purposes:- that is, cross-fire would be so directed as to
force our troops to concentrate in a given area - the moment such a
concentration had been effected, mortars would open fire for effect.

3. Both NCOs found that they were rapidly and effectively engaged by
mortars wherever they were. It was noted that mortar fire followed
them accurately as they moved, in spite of the fact that they could
not be seen from the mortar position. This is attributed by the NCOs
to efficient enemy communications. Spotters had been placed in a
large number of buildings. These buildings were connected by direct
lines to the various mortar and MG posts. As a result and the
detailed range-cards, it was possible for enemy mortars to keep up
constant and effective fire wherever our troops moved. Both NCOs most
strongly urge that one of the first things to do is to look for and
cut wires. When they did discover field phone wires and cut these,
they immediately found enemy fire to become far less accurate.

4. The NCOs believe that the actual number of troops used by the enemy
in defence of POURVILLE was small - probably not more than a hundred
men; and the enemy success was due largely to the excellent siting of
mortars and MG posts, which effectively covered all approaches and
were so disposed as to allow of a maximum of cross-fire at most points.
Heavier enemy mortars constantly out-ranged ours, and the NCOs also
believe that the enemy's automatic weapons were faster than ours.

5. Another comment made is that the pill-boxes and concrete emplace-
ments of the enemy were so well constructed that our mortar fire,
despite considerable accuracy, remained ineffective.

6. French Civilians - The NCOs commented on the great friendliness of
the French civilians. A number of them had packed necessaries, in the
hope of fleeing to England, to join the Fighting French. They cite
the example of one sixteen-year old -

Debriefing of Sgt Hawkins and Jack after the Dieppe raid P.1

boy who came from the hills to join our Forces. He displayed
marks on his wrists where he had been slashed by the Germans
for allegedly not working hard enough.

A touch of humour in a very serious situation was the case
of several of our snipers firing from civilian houses where
beds had been placed against windows while French girls fed
them wine and cakes.

French civilians stated that the Germans started intensive
fortification of the area approximately 4/5 weeks ago. For
this purpose civilians of the German "TODT" Organization and
Flemish workers had been imported.

It is interesting to note that French civilians were well
aware of the fact that this was a raid and not an invasion.
Our troops, according to the NCOs, constantly urged civilians
to seek safety and not expose themselves to Hun reprisals.
The enthusiasm of the French, however, was so great that
they seemed to disregard personal danger.

7. <u>Morale and Heroism</u> — Both NCOs stated that the morale of
our troops remained high throughout,
Even when they were making their 'last stand' on the beach
and fully realized that their chances of returning were slim
they kept fighting extremely hard and always found time to
crack the odd joke and encourage each other. One example of
outstanding heroism is quoted:

"A young private of the S S R who was manning a light mortar
had been firing from cover. He was eventually hit, receiving
four MG wounds in the stomach. He turned to his comrades and
said 'I got it, boys,' picked up the mortar, took it out into
the open in order to engage the enemy post more effectively
and scored several hits before he died."

Comments: Both Sgt. HAWKINS and F/Sgt NISSENTHALL are intelligent and keen soldiers. It is obvious that they
kept their eyes and ears open and it is respectfully submitted
that a thorough interrogation of these NCOs by battle school
instructors would be valuable.

Interviewed by

(P. Lieven)
G.S.O.3(I).   Capt.

Adv H.Q., 1 Cdn Corps,
22 Aug 42.

Copies to:

Corps Comd.
B.G.S.
D.A. & Q.M.G.

Debriefing of Sgt Hawkins and Jack after the Dieppe raid P.2

Report on the Dieppe Raid by Lieut H MacMillan dated 27 August 1942.

In the last paragraph on page two he wrote:

(a) The Germans seemed to use their mortar and machine guns conjunctively. With the M.Gs they forced us to take cover and then they opened up on us with the mortar. This proved very effective and very deadly. The German mortar fire was very accurate. In conjunction with these two weapons, the Germans seemed to have kept a close watch on our movements by means of spotters who must have been in telephone communication with the guns. This enabled them to fire on us when we were in forest areas quite out of sight of the guns. The spotters were in houses and buildings all over the area from the way that they were able to follow our movements. The mistake that was made was in not cutting all the telephone wires in the first phase of the battle. We did cut some on the return trip to the beaches and there was a noticeable decrease in the number of mortar bombs that came near us. F/Sgt Nissenthall reports that in his estimation the wires could only have been up for a month.

OSOIII(I),
HQ, 2 Cdn Div.

DIEPPE RAID

1. I submit the following report.

2. Accompanied by B.25107, A/Sgt. Skippon, E.K., of this Section, I boarded L.C.T. #8 at NEWHAVEN on the evening, 18 Aug 42. Nothing to report until approx. 0400 hrs., 19 Aug 42, when we could see the flares dropped by our aircraft and hear loud explosions coming from the land ahead of us. There was a very heavy Naval bombardment from our escorting ships and as we came closer to land, we were subjected to intense fire from machine guns, A.A. Batteries, and lt. Arty. Batteries.

3. L.C.T. #8 touched down on the beach in front of the tobacco factory at 0510 hrs. (approx.). Fire was so intense that the Engineers were unable to lay the wooden tracks for the tanks. One tank under Capt. Stanton did however succeed in landing but was unable to go further than the beach, being stuck by the deep shale and pebbles in the tracks. As the fire from the land became hotter and after receiving hits, our craft withdrew from the beach and attempted to land again four to five hundred yards further along towards White Beach, where an attempt was made to land another tank under the command of Lieut.-Col. Andrews. This tank landed in deep water where it apparently became swamped, as it did not move any further. We had to withdraw again. While withdrawing, our steering gear was hit, causing us to go around in circles some four or five hundred yards off shore where the enemy seemed to do his utmost to destroy us, finally stopping our engines, causing us to lay with our open prow towards the shore. While we lay facing the shore, under terrific fire from the enemy, a shell hit the tank carrying hydrogen gas for our barrage balloon, setting them on fire.

4. A/Sgt. Skippon, 2 Cdn F.S. Sec. wrapped a blanket around the fire and with the assistance of others, succeeded in throwing it overboard.

5. At about 0830 hrs, 19 Aug 42, while still laying in this exposed position under enemy fire, orders were given to throw Engineers High Explosive, Plastic H.E., overboard. As no one appeared to organize this party, I took charge, and with an Engineer Sgt. and a Sapper carried the P.H.E. out to the front of the ship and dropped it overboard.

6. As soon as the enemy saw men appear, he tried to hit us with machine gun fire; no one was hit. On returning to the back of the platform, I looked around and noticed one bundle of P.H.E. had NOT gone overboard but had become jammed between the platform, and the platform cable. I returned and managed to kick it loose and throw it into the sea. By this time our Engine room and bridge had been hit causing considerable casualties. My next task was to convey messages from Brig. Lett, who was wounded, lying on a stretcher between a tank and a recce. car at the rear of the ship. The messages had to be passed over the top to Lieut.-Col. King, who was endeavouring to organize volunteers to operate the Diesel Engines.

7. The enemy seemed to have everything in sight very well covered, and an attempt was made to get anyone who so much as made an appearance.

8. Shortly after this we were given a tow some distance out to sea where a French chasseur came alongside and took some of our wounded aboard; finally one of H.M. Sloops took us in tow.

9. The last offensive action by the enemy was taken by a Dornier plane some 12 miles from England. The sloop fired at this plane which veered off; another ship must have hit it as it appeared to be on fire. It unloaded its bombs in the sea.

Report by Lt MacMillan page 1

10. Just before this last action took place, Lieut.-Col. McTavish, ?CE, Capt. Inainger, I.O., 2 Cdn Div., Lieut. Fairweather and an O.R. from the 14th Tank Bn., with six others, were buried at sea by the Commander of the Sloop.

11. Brig. Lett and Lieut.-Col. King both acted in a very cool manner and were an inspiration to all aboard.

12. The above is a resume of the happening aboard L.C.T. 8.

13. The following report was submitted by N.15968 Sgt. Hawkins, R., 11 Cdn F.S. Sec. and P/Sgt. Nissenthall, J., R.D.F. expert from the R.A.F., who made a joint verbal report to the G.S.O.III(I), 1 Cdn Corps. -

"From Southampton we proceeded to Dieppe where we were landed on GREEN beach at 0445 hrs. 19 Aug 42. We met with no opposition and to my knowledge it would seem to have been a surprise landing. Within twenty minutes (approx) however we came under fire from machine guns. During this time a few civilians were rounded up, one of which was German. I searched this chap but found nothing on him so I turned him over to the South Sask. Regt. to deal with as they saw fit.

"The M.G. fire met with in the first period of the battle held up the company that was to proceed to the R.D.F. station so Nissenthall and myself attached ourselves to the Camerons who were proceeding inland to the airport. We hoped in this way to eventually reach our objective by a detour.

"It was while we were moving inland with the Camerons that I met Sgt. Corson of your Section. He was okay at that time.

"After putting up with an overcoming much M. G. and mortar fire, we arrived at a spot about four miles inland. It was now approx. 0930 hrs. It was at this point that we received a wireless message telling us that the evacuation boats would be at the beaches to pick us up at 1100 hrs. so we had to turn about and head for the beach.

"On the return journey we had with us a German prisoner who had been captured just before we were advised to return. This prisoner was never brought back to England as he was left on the beach when we had to make a run for the boats.

"We made a stand in an empty hotel near the beach and waited for the boats. It was here that we suffered considerable casualties.

"At approx. 1200 hrs. we boarded a boat and started on the return trip to NEWHAVEN where we were landed at 0300 hrs. 20 Aug 42.

"During our stay on the continent we were at no time able to reach any of the objectives set for us. We did however notice the following things -

(a) The Germans seemed to use their mortar and machine guns conjunctively. With the M.Gs they forced us to take cover and then they opened up on us with the mortar. This proved very effective and very deadly. The German mortar fire was very accurate. In conjunction with these two weapons, the Germans seemed to have kept a close watch on our movements by means of spotters who must have been in telephonic communication with the guns. This enabled them to fire on us when we were in forest areas quite out of sight of the guns. The spotters were in houses and buildings all over the area from the way that they were able to follow our movements. The mistake that was made was in not cutting all the telephone wires in the first phase of the battle. We did cut some on the return trip to the beaches and there was a noticeable

Report by Lt Macmillan page 2

212

decrease in the number of mortar bombs that came near us. F/Sgt Nissenthall reports that in his estimation the wires could only have been up for a month.

(b) It is the idea of all that in future raids valuable help could be made of aircraft in the knocking out of M.G. nests and mortars, the positions of which could be passed to the aircraft by radio, if there, such arrangements were made. It would seem that close contact between the Air Force and the forward fighting troops would ease numerous situations, such as arose on our part of the coast.

(c) Many also maintained that had we been in possession of light artillery, we could have overcome all the M.G. Pill boxes. The mortars we had seemed to have little effect on them whatsoever.

(d) The French civilians were very friendly and crowded down to the beach hoping that we would be able to take them back to England. They were extremely calm even in the face of fierce fighting. One young lad of 16 or 17 years had slash marks on his wrists. He claimed that he had received these at the hands of the Germans because he had refused to work in the fields for them. The civilians as a whole realized that it was a raid and not an invasion.

<u>MORALE</u>

"I report this under a separate heading because to my knowledge it warrants it. The troops were at all times in the very best of spirits even in the worst of conditions. I saw no lagging nor any desire but to fight and fight to the last. In every case where they came to grips with the Germans, they showed great courage and fighting spirit."

14. For your information.

(H. MacMillan)   Lieut.
O. C., 2 Cdn F. S. Sec.

I was given permission and warrant to return to London on the early morning workers' train.

Later that morning I made my way to Air Ministry for an interview with AVM Victor Tait, to whom I had described my activities of the previous day. He was more than relieved that I had not been killed as had been reported.

Chapter Twelve: A secret mission worth £4.0s.0d.

Jack's return home on 20 August 1942, is well-documented by my family. My mother (his fiancée) said my father was "drunk" from what she called "stay awake" pills. She removed shrapnel from his leg. I also have a marvellous video of my uncle Julius, made in 2019, describing Jack in assorted bits of uniform arriving at 39 Teesdale Street (which Jack considered to be home) and how Jack slept for twenty-four hours.

Julius also wrote in 2019:

"He came to Teesdale Street ex Dieppe, dressed in battledress, unshaven and asked to use my bed and collapsed on it. He was absolutely exhausted. We all loved him so very much."

My mother's youngest brother, Frankie, who lives in Los Angeles now, has sent me a page from his diary that he wrote at the age of nine.

When I came home from school yesterday afternoon I had a cup of tea and a piece of bread and butter. At 7 o' clock p.m. I came in, and my surprise was my brother-in-law [actually his future brother-in-law]. When he last came home he had three stripes, but now he has three stripes and a crown. My brother-in-law had been over to Dieppe. But still I must not tell any more because car[e]less talk costs lives and will not bring VICTORY."

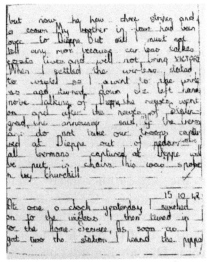

Frankie's War diary page 1

Frankie's War diary page 2

Another interesting and important scrap of paper was happily discovered by my cousin among his late father's belongings. It is now in the archive at the Jewish Museum London.

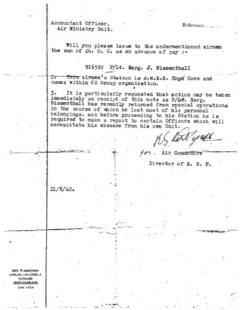

£4. 0s. 0d. as an advance of pay given to Jack so he could replace the uniform he had 'lost' during the Dieppe Raid.

Account Officer,
Air Ministry Unit,

Will you please issue undermentioned airman the sum of £4.0.0. as an advance of pay:-

916592 F/Lt. Serg. J. Nissenthall

2. This airman's station is A.M.E.S. Hope Cove and comes within 60 Group organisation.

3. It is particularly requested that action may be taken immediately on receipt of this note as F/Serg. Nissenthall has recently returned from special operations, in the course of which he lost most of his personal belongings, and before proceeding to his Station he is required to make a report to certain Officers which will necessitate his absence from his own Unit.

(Signed) for Air Commodore
Director of R.D.F
21/8/42

Jack goes to be debriefed by his mentor Dr Jones.

Feeling greatly refreshed after almost twenty-four hours continuous sleep, I made my way to Dr Jones' secret headquarters, in a rather dingy building overlooking the Thames near Westminster. After being cleared by various security executives I finally arrived at his office, the walls of which were now decorated with maps showing the positions of a fund of new radio devices, communication systems and most important of all, German radar plots that had come to light during the hectic operations of Dieppe day.

Overnight we had received a complete picture of the operational organisation of the German defence in Northern France. By cunning subterfuge, they had concealed from us most of their inadequacies. Their excellent defensive tactics also demonstrated to our military planners what prodigious efforts would be required to give the D-Day landings a reasonable chance of success. Though D-Day was, it must be remembered, still two years ahead, it was quite obvious that every minute would be required to prepare the correct equipment and train the men for the massive combined operation which dare not fail.

Before Dieppe, skilful use of the radio telephone systems by the Luftwaffe ground control had given us a completely false impression of the enemy's air strength in Northern France and the Low Countries. Many different call signs were used by any one fighter squadron, leaving our intelligence services to assess their defensive strength as far greater than it actually was in practice. Dieppe called their bluff. Aircraft were heard being routed from the Low Countries, and even from Germany to assist in the invasion. After Dieppe, our fighter sweeps were stepped up accordingly, and from then on the air over France was made as untenable for the Luftwaffe as sections of the Kent countryside had at times been for the RAF some two years previously. The cycle had been completed and in two years the pendulum had swung and the German air force problems of 1940 to 41 were now ours in 1942.

During the night blitz, Goering had lost many a

sleepless night as no answer could be found to the steadily increasing nightly losses of his bombers. In 1942 we were saddled with the self-same problem, but now, after Dieppe, we had the clues to the answers. In May and June 1942 the first of the thousand bomber raids had been marked by uneconomical heavy RAF losses. Since January of that year, the German night defences had been improved immeasurably, as we knew only too well, but exactly what had been done to obtain the improved results was not known. Apart from the quizzing of returning bombing crews lucky enough to have survived a German night fighter attack, and the radio eavesdropping of instructions issued by the Luftwaffe, to their night fighter controllers, there was no substantial method of obtaining intelligence information on German radar defence. Now, after Dieppe, we realised that their success was almost entirely due to their excellent ground organisation and not to the performance of their radar equipment.

Methods would have to be found to confound and confuse German ground control operators.

When, during the operation, the telephone communication to the German radio stations was interrupted, the Dieppe radar operators had no option but to go on to plain language radio plotting, using their emergency wireless broadcasting system.

The missing clue of the German night successes became immediately apparent. Dr Jones's eavesdroppers waiting in England recorded all the transmitted information, and found the German aircraft plotting to be extraordinarily accurate even under the saturation conditions indicated on their indicator tubes on Dieppe day.

However in daytime the Germans' radar screen must have presented very much the same kind of picture as during any of the large-scale night raids now being carried out on the hinterland of Germany. The masses of German radar plots which had been recorded were being individually plotted on a series of large war maps in England. These now hung in Dr Jones' office. It was in this self-same historic office later in the war that Dr Jones became the first man to positively identify the V2. It showed that the German radar operators were excellently trained, and their proficiency with their short-range narrow beam radars allow them to easily cope with an enormous number of tracks simultaneously.

As a result radar jamming of an extreme kind was then prepared for future use by a special RAF force under Dr Cockburn. To confuse the German operators during our night raids, radio counter-measures aircraft were prepared with a large variety of jamming equipment working on the frequencies of the various German radars used in the defence of the Reich. Strangely enough, and despite the advice of Dr Jones, their use was delayed for months, causing gradually increasing losses to our bomber force. Eventually, with the use of various jamming devices, including "Window" [radar jamming caused by dropping foil strips from aircraft] and the annoying and frustrating mimicking of German ground controllers' voices by special German-speaking RAF radio countermeasures operators, sometimes even flying in the attacking aircraft, life became increasingly unhappy for the man in charge of German night defence. Misleading instructions issued to the Luftwaffe night fighters by the RCM [Radio Counter Measures] radio telephone operators caused the German night fighters to be sent on wild goose chases across the cold night skies. At times the German ground controllers could be heard pleading with their night fighter pilots to obey their instructions and not those of the airborne radio saboteurs. Often the efforts of the RCM operators brought the German controllers to a point of near apoplexy. Needless to say, the RCM operators thoroughly enjoyed their work.

Militarily, the Dieppe Raid was an invaluable, constructive but extremely costly reconnaissance in force. Many years later it is easy from the comfort of an armchair to criticise Operation Jubilee, with a pile of references conveniently at your elbow and a glass of wine in your hand. At that time, however, our aim and object was to attack the enemy with enough force to make him even to a small degree divide his war effort. Also, to sit back and wait was not enough for the men who had suffered so much at the time of Dunkirk. Nobody expected a picnic and despite the sneers of some present-day critics, I think I speak for the vast majority of the men of Dieppe when I say that we are fiercely proud of having taken part in that bloody, heroic but intensely instructive debacle. It has been said that each Canadian death at Dieppe saved at least ten men on D-Day.

Many pet theories held by the Allied planners before Dieppe were proved dangerously incorrect and much rethinking was needed in order to come up with the right answers to the problem of landing an army on the continent. The Chief of Combined Operations, Admiral Lord Louis Mountbatten, called a conference immediately after the raid. All executive officers engaged in the operation were called upon to say their piece without pulling their punches. As a result of these hectic interludes the initial plans for the D-Day operation were formulated. Instead of attempting to take a harbour by force, design and construction began immediately on the component parts of the transportable prefabricated 'Mulberry' harbour. The need for an intense pre-landing bombardment was accepted. Exact timing and complete reliance on surprise was ruled out of any future large-scale landing operations.

As a postscript to this I would like to include a transcript of a videoed conversation Jack had with Don Preist fifty years after the Dieppe raid.

Don Preist, the brilliant radar scientist, and Jack first met before the Second World War when they were both working at Bawdsey, the early radar research establishment, Don as a scientist and the younger Jack as a volunteer. It was a friendship that continued throughout the war. The only person Jack was permitted to visit prior to the Dieppe Raid was Don who had been transferred to TRE (Telecommunications and Radar Establishment) at Malvern.

When Jack asked Don what should be his priority once he reached the German radar station, Don replied with another question. "What do you consider the most important thing in your radar station? What would you miss most if attacked?"

Jack thought for a moment, then said, "Our telephone."

Don replied, "Well that's what you have to disable as soon as you can."

Their friendship endured for the remainder of their lives. In a video interview made in 1992 when Jack visited Don in California, Jack said that Don's work on Oboe (an accurate, all-weather bomb-aiming system) and developing the equipment to disable the German Wurzburg radar system had saved countless pilots' lives. In response Don said of Jack's actions at Dieppe that they had been invaluable.

Don: "When Jack came to see me at Malvern not long after the Bruneval raid, we shared a cup of tea and [a] chat and he told me what it was that he was about to do. I was horrified - suitably horrified, actually - and I would've been even more horrified if I'd known the whole story. He came to see if I had any suggestions about what to do when he got to his objective and I would've said practically nothing of any value whatsoever. I probably gave him encouragement and [remarked], "It will be a piece of cake" or some such nonsense."[8]

Jack: "It was in the Winter Gardens in Malvern. We had tea and pastries. Remember? You bought my tea."

Don: "Did I buy your tea? Your tea. (He chuckles). Well, Jack, here we are together after all these years. What will you be saying after all this?"

Jack: "You saved so many of our bomber boys' lives in the bombing over Germany when you defeated the Wurzburg radar."

Don: "I had a small part but that was a very successful thing. I was proud to be in on it; part of it."

Don then responded by saying, "And now let's drink a toast to you Jack, because of what you did in your operation and the use of Mandrel[9] resulted in the saving of large numbers of lives on D-Day. That was your contribution."

"Cheers" they both said, "Good luck."

---

[8] The Bruneval Raid, Operation Biting, took place February 1942. Paratroopers attacked a Wurzburg Radar station on the north French coast and took much of the radar equipment to the boats waiting for them on the beach below. Don Preist was waiting for them in one of the boats, and from what he gleaned from talking to the soldiers, and examining the equipment, was able with his team at TRE to develop a jamming device which disabled the Wurzburg radar system during bombing raids over Germany.

[9] Mandrel was a radar jamming device developed by the scientists and technicians working at TRE Malvern, using the information gleaned from the German radio transmissions and Jack's observations of the German Freya radar station.

Chapter Thirteen: Onwards to the Middle East

In September 1942, after the Dieppe Raid, Jack went back to Hope Cove. From there he continued his prolific letter-writing to his girlfriend Dally.

On the first day of September, only twelve days after the Dieppe Raid, it is striking how mundane his first letter is, with his usual complaint about the pile of work awaiting him, and grumbling about the lack of intelligence of his staff.

Jack goes about his duties and responsibilities, much as usual.

One important component of his pre-war life had been his attachment to aspects of Jewish communal life. In one letter he describes how his old Hebrew teacher from Teesdale Street Talmud Torah Hebrew School appears in uniform. At first they did not recognise one another, but when they did, Jack organised for some Jewish servicemen to attend a service in Torquay. He was all set to accompany them, when, as often happened,

> My apparatus started to have a baby [needed to be repaired]…….. I missed a very interesting evening at my second (or it would have been) Jewish service during the war.

There was a mechanical problem with the radar apparatus, so he could not go to the service with his men.

On 9 January 1943 Jack writes that as soon as his friend Jim Henderson is back from hospital (after a head injury),

> I'm going to Exminster which is a suburb of Exeter. It's a station of a type which is important, but has been completely mismanaged. My job will be to clear it up. Organising inefficient mechanics and operators, it's just the job I want to wake me up. Something to get my teeth into. I'll still be in charge of this dump [affectionate name for Bolt Head!] by remote control and it is going to work out perfectly. Bags of opportunities for initiative and unlimited powers.

Jack spent a short period back at Yatesbury and was later sent to West Kirby, near Liverpool. His next orders from above saw him embark on the long journey by ship, around the Cape of Good Hope. He could not divulge his destination. His journey from Liverpool to Port Said, was the longest rest he had during the war. It would have been far too dangerous to take the short route via Gibraltar and into the Mediterranean. That route was full of enemy submarines and mines. He quite enjoyed it, with good food, plenty of fresh air and exercise, and was accompanied by a few of his radar friends.

916592 FS Nissenthall
A9704
HQ RAF
APO 3980
19/3/43

My Dear Dally,

My address looks pretty clear but I'm hoping your letters reach me with only a little delay.

It seems that I am going to be cut off from any ordinary connections with home civilisation for a little while.

Please don't worry and try to restrain other people because I'm on a sissy job. It's not at all dashing. The worst part will be the boredom of waiting for precisely nothing. I'm going to find that harder than all the long hours of duty I have put in the last few years.

As I told you in my last "note", I'm on a ship. It's extremely nice and I'm feeling really fit for the first time for quite a period.

Though I'm not much of a sailor I'm not doing too bad. I haven't been seasick and so far, I have felt quite happy. Conditions are quite okay, food reasonable and the air is worth one million. I've got an idea that I'm homesick already, but I suppose I will have to get over that.

I've started using your picture again as a stomach lifter [to raise his spirits]. It works so well. As far as I can make out the most important thing in life is to get this war over, and settle down to a normal peaceful existence; with ordinary imaginary grievances to grumble about and no binding [RAF slang for grumbling] waiting to upset. I've been waiting for years now.

I suppose the saying that apples at the top of the tree are sweeter is very apt. I am sure that is my consolation to no one.

Every time I come home I found that I seem to be living an alien existence.

My mother is trying very hard at Mattock Lane, but what I want to come home to is some of my very own home comforts[10].

I hope you see what I mean. It annoys me to have to get out, [in order] to have to enjoy any quiet and privacy.

At times it makes me feel sick and tired. By now I should easily have had a place of my own, with all the things I've dreamed about.

Every time I get home however it gives me a nasty jolt. Well my plans have been very simple after this do.

I suppose we'll have to start a long-distance correspondence chain for a while. [He didn't know it would be three years before he saw

---

[10] His mother was eventually settled at Mattock Lane, Ealing, after being evacuated initially to Cosford, Cambridgeshire, and then Stalybridge, Lancashire.

Dally again.] Please don't lose heart because I'm sure it won't be long now.

I've got Cliff Robinson [a fellow radar engineer] here with me now, he is also writing. Seems that he's got plenty to write about too.

Don't like the fact that I won't even be able to hear you for a time, but it's the fault of that rat Hitler.

Perhaps you can have realised that I was moving, by my many phone messages.

Incidentally at the very last moment, I managed to get my sleeping bag, the paper was all torn and your note or letter was gone but I received the bag.

Believe me, Dally, it's been a wonderful asset at the times I needed it.

I don't know how I'm going to send you the bobs [shillings] but I'll make it up.

Well Dally I'll say good night now.

I'm going out on deck to get a breath of air.

All my love

Jack

xxxxxx

En route, they stopped at Durban, and the warm welcome he received there, as well as the sunshine, sowed the seed for his eventual emigration to South Africa. He spoke with enthusiasm about the hospitality of the locals. He had very fond memories of this.

An enigmatic letter comes in May from a numbered address. It includes a statement of why he is fighting the war.

916582
A9704 RAF
c/o AP0 3980
April/May 1943

My Dear Dally,

It's only a short time since I posted my previous letter but I've just managed to get an address verified. You may write to the above address. Better quote Army Post Office instead of APO.

Don't get worried if I don't reply for some time. The letter will most likely chase me for some time. This pen seems rather erratic, I'm not putting anything in Italics. It's this nib.

I suppose you are very suspicious as to what's taking place, all this letter writing etc.

Well it's just that I'm travelling a bit farther than usual. Also I suppose I'll be away as long as ever I have been before.

Though I don't think the period will be exceptionally long.

You might think that I am treating this enforced absence too lightly.

My feelings are that there is a job yet to be done, and without its full completion life would be intolerable for all the Jewish people.

I'm only playing a little part, admittedly, but I feel I can do it well and in no little way help to end this bundle."

He ends by saying

Perhaps you might be kind enough to tell mum or rather hint that I am on a ship going some place where I'm going to have some fun. Safe fun this time.
That is so near enough the truth. Please do you what you can.
My next letter will take a while to get to you but it will be very important.

all my love
Jack
xxx
xxx
xxx

It is a sign of his faith in Dally's empathy, that he gives her the task of telling his mother he is on a ship somewhere.

They arrive at Port Said. His letters now are censored. It is quite easy to observe the change of tone.

Jack in front of the canteen, Helwan, Egypt 1943

Jack wrote a note on the reverse which reads:

Outside our canteen. The canteen is now under sea. Jack

Miss Adelaide Bernard
39 Teesdale Street
London E2
England

9th May 1943

A9704

916592 Nissenthall

F/S RAF H/Q

APO 3980

My dear Dally,

It's some time since I have been able to write but I assure you I have not been wasting time. In fact I've been having the time of my life.

The trip out here was speedy and happy and I arrived in the very best of health. Since then I have been lucky enough to have bags of exercise and sunshine and right now I'm as fit as I have ever been. There is nothing much I can tell you except that my boys are about the best one could ever expect. As soon as present excitement dies down, I'm going to get a mass photograph and send it to you. You'll see what a load of twerps they are.

Our main occupation of the moment is resting and sleeping, both of which are right in my line. Please give my regards to everybody especially your father and mother.

Love, Jack xxx

Jack with some of his team at Helwan, 1943

A telegram is sent:

29 June 1943

Miss Adelaide Bernard
39 Teesdale Street
London E2

Letter and telegram received many thanks you
are more than ever in my thoughts at this time
All my love
Jack Nissentall

According to a letter written on 24 July 1943 soon
after his arrival in Egypt, Jack visited the Jewish club
who were welcoming "rookies".

Whilst at the club I was presented with a parcel
of useful gear made up in Palestine. There was

an amazing selection of useful things.

To give you some idea, there was shaving soap, toilet soap, toothpaste, writing pad, pencil, silk vest, pants, handkerchief, cigarettes, matches, nuts, raisins. There was also sweets and many other things but I can't just remember them now.

It certainly was very nice, but I am in no way short of any of the various items.

Jack installed and operated an 800 type GCI at El Gamil, the airport at Port Said, in preparation for the Sicily landings. This is also where the British paratroops landed during the Suez Campaign.

In September 1943 he helped in setting up a radar school for training GCI instructors at Helwan, near Cairo. In November that year he trained crews for microwave type 14 and GCI at Algiers following the invasion of Sicily and Italy.

On the 30 December 1943 he writes

Please excuse the long delay since my last communication! I have been living a rather unsettled literary existence, in that I've been doing a lot of writing, but on technical topics.

Moreover the food was good, "little different from what we have [used to have] at home". By comparison with the locals his food and accommodation were good.

In 1944, his letters would describe the appalling conditions in which the locals lived, and the filth.

Almost where ever you go in the native localities you see evidence of the worlds worst diseases. The squalor and filth of the average person's existence is [sic] indescribable. Near my present camp is a large collection of shacks which have been constructed in the usual Egyptian custom, without roofs! water or sanitation. There is more dirt in this part of the universe than any place I know. The odours drift if the wind is favourable (wrong adjective) onto our road to town. I make a point of indulging in as little breathing as possible, whilst passing.

This place is typical of most other typical native towns. The smell increases to the square of the heat.

Then he has experience of extreme cold and floods.

January 30, 1944

It is getting distinctly cold these days and I'm considering the prospect of sorting out my winter woollies. For some time now we have been bothered by much wind and rain but we are reasonably well protected against mother nature.

The unfortunate part of our location is that we are about 0 feet above sea level and when it rains it takes some time for the rain to sink through the sand. Consequently we spend the odd day also paddling away to and from our technical site.

Still we can't grumble because some people are really roughing it. If ever I feel cold I think of the period I spent sleeping on a landing craft with one blanket and groundsheet. Those days are past and my present life is one of comparative luxury.

There are periods of extreme danger from what he calls "nasty disease" I presume he means diseases from lack of hygiene and clean water, such as cholera, dysentery and malaria. 130,000 died from malaria[11] at that time. When things are particularly bad, the men are advised not to go to the local cinema or to frequent local cafes.

At one point they are told their post home will be delayed by two weeks because of "disease" (probably it was fumigated before being put on a plane back to England). For this reason, their carefully numbered letters[12] were sometimes out of order.

He continuously complains of the stench. Besides, the disease, they were also plagued by midges, flies and of course malarial mosquitos.

Jack prided himself on making insect protection for the openings of his tent. However, no sooner was he settled in one place than he was moved on to another. Once he was housed in a wooden chalet, but preferred the tent because of the air movement.

---

[11] *Egypt's Other Wars: Epidemics and the Politics of Public Health* by Nancy Elizabeth Gallagher, Syracuse University Press 1990.

[12] Jack and Dally agree to number their letters so that they would know in what order to read them.

Jock Gordon in their compound which had been flooded when the sea wall was breached.

One night, in February 1944, the sea wall was breached and they were flooded at 2.30 in the morning. They had to rush to save their equipment and belongings, but the water was deep.

It came over the top of our gumboots.

I managed to get all kit on board some lorries and hurried to a safer location. The next and actually the most important job was to make tea. That is always the matter of greatest precedence.

At any time in the presence of work relaxes, we make tea. By the time we had organised tea, the sea had found its level. This was such that gumboots were useless. We still wore them, however, because it helps to keep the mud out of your toes. Well, we had our chai and a singsong and then dawn broke. We then got organised and moved off to a drier site.

Despite all this, he tried to make himself as comfortable as possible, with pictures of Dally about the place, and as communication with the outside world was most important, he says:

Incidentally I have made a horrible little radio that gets home programmes very nicely so I will never be short of home news.

And indeed he keeps up with the news with his radio. He worries constantly about Dally's (and the rest of the family's) wellbeing.

This new robot bombing[13] is a rehash of Big Bertha in the last war. Only trouble is that it is London now, not Paris and the range is 150 miles not 75. I wish you all and mum would get out of London. Surely you can organise something. Of course it's just like your pop and Julius to keep out of shelter. Personally, I don't mind bullets or shrapnel etc when you know where it's coming from and can do something about it.

But blind, or semi-blind shelling is definitely deadly. Right now I'm living in comparative safety, but I'm always worrying about you ones back home.

---

[13] V1 flying bombs, as known as doodle-bugs

On a few occasions I have been in some danger but nowhere near as much as some people back home.

Before we know where we are, the Russians will be at the gates to Berlin, and we should be able to meet them from the other side.

From a distance it is all very thrilling, but the going must be pretty grim in France.

Getting back to his everyday life in Egypt, he tells Dally, the food was more than passable:

Actually the food is little different to what we have at home. Food is normally fine and of reasonable quality. The meat is sometimes a trifle high, but at least we get meat. Potatoes are usually of the sweet variety but every so often we get some real ones.

The cooking is usually first class in the mess, and pastry is always hundred per cent.

Jack Nissenthall (second from right) has become something of a super hero in wake of recent disclosures concerning his daring World War II activities. A. A. Goldes, who snapped this photo near Port Said, Egypt, is now a resident of Toronto. Says Goldes, "Nissenthall was a real whiz kid ... very modest and brave."

Jack and some of his team at Helwan, Egypt 1943 in front of the same hut and Crossley lorry.
Clipping from Canadian Jewish Veterans news-sheet

Dally sends him parcels when she is able. He requests some "odds and ends":

Number One is toothpowder, and Number Two is plain common or garden black boot polish. This might seem a queer request, but shoes get awfully muddy here. I've used up my ration.

In March 1944 a parcel arrives….

Your long-awaited parcel has arrived together with number 20 [letter]. This is my lucky day. The items you sent were just what I really want.

Smelling Wright's Coal Tar has made me really

homesick. That is the brand the mater used way back. I'm thinking of keeping them (the bars of soap). It's to counteract the unhealthy smells we get around this part of the world.

The shaving cream looks and smells good. I'll tell you what it's like tomorrow. Then, of course, you have also managed to get some of my favourite toothpaste. It was unobtainable when I left England. Just how much trouble did you go to, to obtain these things. I don't want you hoofing all around London to get my odds and ends? It is possible to get the necessaries of living without having to make you wear your feet out?

I must admit that the parcel made contact with home and supplements your beautiful letters.

There is no doubt about it I'm getting a trifle homesick.

One of Jack's enjoyments had always been swimming and he went swimming in the Mediterranean whenever he could. I remember him telling me that he and his mates would frequently play with dolphins. They became extremely tame and were great fun. One day the same dolphins became very rough and kept pushing them over. It became uncomfortable …so much so, that he and his fellow swimmers left the sea, only to see a shark had been coming towards them. Jack was convinced the dolphins had been protecting them.

*Jack adjusting an aerial on top of the barbed wire perimeter
fence. Egypt 1943.*

Chapter Fourteen: Homesickness malaria floods

The extremes of temperature in Egypt were a problem. Life was uncomfortable for most of the time.

You see the weather here is subject to terrific variation in temperature. During the day the temperature stays at sixty degrees which I now find cold. To give you some idea, I wear my service jersey and another pullover all day every day. In the evening the temperature drops to below zero at nine o'clock. If you are sitting around doing no exercise you get a chill on the stomach.

You've no idea what a job it is trying to write a letter with gnats, flies, mice and mosquitoes nibbling at you.

Some lads who had spent a spell in the Far East, who were here last year said that there were more species of vermin in this part of the world than in the jungle.

I don't doubt it. All these bloody annoyances try to get their evening meal off me just as I am trying to write a letter.

Every so often I have to lash out at a fly with the old swat. And then a dirty mosquito gets up my trouser leg. Invariably a female too! Still at least we haven't much in the way of bombs and all. To write a letter, which I have to do in the evening, I have to wear an overcoat.... ...Most of the lads get happy in order to keep going at all. Myself I can't stomach the horrible liquor, so I stay in the tent. The warmest place in the tent is bed and that is where I spend most of my spare time.

His description of malaria in the letters sounds harrowing. At first he makes light of it, but gradually the seriousness of the situation is revealed. He told me the long scar on the palm of his hand was from letting it fall on the ground as he was lying on the hospital camp bed, when he was ill, and a scorpion stinging him. It had to be cut to expel the poison. I can still picture that scar, I used to run my fingers over it as a child, and imagine his hand dangling in the sand only to be attacked by a scorpion. In South Africa he used to have recurrences of malaria when I was a child. It seemed to stop as he grew older, and he, not being one to complain, I as a child did not think much of it. He would stay in bed for a couple of days and then be fit as a fiddle after that.

After doing my little bit, I developed something nasty. Please don't let your imagination bring back memories of malaria in the pictures, but I had a wee dose of malaria.

Personally all I had was a nasty headache and high-temperature but you should have seen the fuss they made. When I got back to this area after quite a tiring journey, I was in the middle of my real worst attack. I was whipped out to hospital with some lads from No 4 Commando and was subjected to an intensive cooling........

The nurses were quite nice, Palestinian; they

knew their job. Without a minutes delay I was slammed in bed and an iron fireguard placed over, to form a frame over my body (they didn't even have the decency to let me wear my pants). Over this frame they kept putting sheets soaked in spirits to cool me down.

They put the sheets straight over my head too, and then they put on a fan blowing up from my feet and then and in no time I began to feel bloody cold. The fan was playing right up my legs and draft was coming out of my mouth - amazing isn't it? After about five days of artificial cooling, they condescended to release me. I'm still feeling okay, in fact better than I have been for a long time. Needless to say, I still haven't had my leave, and it looks like I won't get it for quite a while. Actually I would like it now but 'c'est la guerre'. I wouldn't have worried you by spilling any beans, but you sounded very peeved at my not writing. In any case I feel you should know though I'd rather my men didn't know.

He did not want his men to know how serious the malaria attacks had been.

9 July 1944

There is no need to worry about the illness I had. It may even help me to go home. If I get it seven times I will be on my way home. That makes five to go. I think I could take it in order to see you again. Time seemed to be going fast last week or two, the work has been simply

247

colossal, but I enjoy it. I'm my own boss now.

He continues to console Dally:

> 17 July 1944
> Incidentally my malaria was not very bad, at least didn't feel bad.
> In fact the discomfort at times, was balanced by the wizard time I had resting afterwards

Eventually Jack is sent to a convalescent camp in Carthage, Tunisia.

> 29 July 1944
> At the moment I'm some 2000 miles away [Carthage, Tunisia] from the place where I have been working and I must say it's a relief. I have no RAF or operational work of any kind to me, I'm just relaxing.
> Once again, I've had a very interesting time but I'm physically and mentally exhausted. As you can sleep as long as you like here, and get tea et cetera in bed, I intend to sleep for two or three days non-stop.

His bid, to cheer Dally up by down-playing the malaria bout was negated by a letter he sent her a few months later.

> 18 Sept 1944
> There is no doubt about it, I have been in a bad way but I didn't really realise it. The German doctor has given me some personal hints on how to deal with the after effects of malaria. His

main idea was that one should eat and eat and eat. Well, I've been doing almost that mainly for want of something better to do.

I'm sorry, darling, I can't tell you any more, but the story though extremely interesting would have been completely blue pencilled [censored] so I'm rather tuckered.

Continuing with his take on the war, later in September 1944 he writes:

It's unbelievable just how well we have progressed on the Continent, it seems almost too good to be true. Well, as I was saying I'm moving out again, this time on leave for a few days. Seemingly there is enough time left for me to get a leave before the European war ends. I'm afraid I'm rather pessimistic with respect to the date of cessation of hostilities with Jerry. They'll be fighting like gangsters in the streets years after the war is over.

On 10 November 1944, he shows his frustration and a touch of bitterness (so unlike him):

Have I a store of ideas for peacetime radar? I'm not giving any more of my ideas away for other gentlemen to use. Only useful ideas for reducing the length of the war and the suffering caused, is what I am writing and thinking about these days. Good ideas I come across during my philosophising, I'm noting for my own post - war benefit. Time has gone when I gave away my brainchildren for other peoples' benefit.

Besides a few official letters of congratulations and a distorted write-up by Quentin Reynolds, [Dress Rehearsal 1943[14]] I have very little to show for my years of inventive hard work.

It's better that way because it seems that people who make the headlines by deed done, invariably make the papers again, but in the obituary. Excuse me binding [RAF slang for whining] Dally but I have some horrible line shoots [unbelievable stories] for our children.

21 Nov 1944

On the basis of my previous record they have collared me for a PT instructor's course lasting about one month, starting December next. Anything that will help to put me back on my feet and make me really fit is just in my line.

The course is a very good holiday in actual fact. It is held in beautiful part of Egypt.

The MO [Medical Officer] here tells me I'm putting on weight steadily, and if I feel like taking this new effort it will help me to regain any original standard of fitness.

He jokes…. "Somebody ought to have told me when I was fit, I didn't know. I'll let you know when I leave here."

On 10 December 1944 Dally is given a window on

---

[14] See Chapter 16

his thoughts on Anti-Semitism in the forces and Britain.

Your optimistic remarks about the happy days about to return were very well received. Everything seems to be pointing that way except two things. Number One, the flying bombs, and Number Two, the release of the Fascists from prison in England. If I know anything about it, we are going to see a spate of anti-Semitic comments. It seems that even now Jews are dodging overseas service and all other forms of dangerous activity, according to the average service man.

The other day I had a very amusing interlude explaining the fallacy to a group of gallant anti-Semites in this part of the world. After making them realise that among us, quite unbeknown to the gentleman I was talking to, there were no fewer than five Jews. The statement was received with the remark that nobody in the mess 'looked like a Jewboy'. I proceeded to enlighten them and then came to Number Five, which is myself. I was very sorry to upset them but they were stunned when I informed them I was a Jew. They couldn't believe it despite my nose and name! Don't think I'm binding [RAF slang for complaining], Dally, but I'm proud of the fact, and I know you feel the same. Now is the time to make these dim types realise they are living in a mediaeval [sic] age with respect to their minds. We're going to have to fight anti-Semitism even in England. For no reason some sections of the forces are rotten with it."

It is quite far-sighted for this twenty-five-year-old airman to have made this prediction in 1944.

A couple of weeks later:

> I went to this Chanucah party. It was for all Jewish personnel but they consisted of mainly Palestinian Jews. Not speaking Hebrew I found the going very hard. It started with a kind of high tea in the open air and then then adjourned to the house for dancing with a Civvie [civilian] band. At that precise time, I decided to depart because I still can't stomach dancing.

He manages a couple of visits to Jerusalem, and obviously enjoys them very much. He writes:

> Also I have just completed seven days' leave in Jerusalem which is a marvellous place.

> The journey was extremely ropey though my reward at the end made it worthwhile. As I told you, I went with Stan Doree who was pleasant company.

> During our cruise across the desert in horrible dry dust with frequent stops at smelly "villages" Stan helped me to maintain consciousness. When we crossed the Egyptian border, the scenery changed completely. Even at the early hours of first light the difference became apparent.

> There were no more dirty stations or dirty

children to bother you. Coming into Palestine we stopped at a model station in some cultivated orange groves. It was just like waking up from a nightmare.

The next stop was Lydda, a town with bags of ancient history.

We changed there onto a local train that was going to do the hour's run to Jerusalem itself.

I managed to get a quick wash, with a bit of a rush, and then piled into the train with a lot of civilians in perfect European dress, with good manners and a very familiar tongue. Hebrew is the universal language, but some of the types spoke Yiddish, which I could almost follow. Luckily I have been studying German for a while. That most certainly helped.

Right opposite Stan and myself were sitting two women with about ten children each. The antics and noise as the mothers proceeded to administer food to the various children was [sic] refreshing. Bananas seemed to be the staple diet for that meal which we enjoyed almost as much as the kids.

When I got to Jerusalem I stayed at service hotels, which incidentally, are very nice indeed.

Good service good food at etc. At a Jewish club there I managed to contact a Jewish family who were kind enough to invite me to their place.

I was lucky enough to have dinner there on two evenings. The old boy was very nice. He comes from Poland via Commercial Road, and we had a good time talking about things in general.

Of course, he is just as English as many other Poles in Great Britain. His wife, however, makes him speak Hebrew, and so when I came, it gave him a chance to relax for a while and speak English.

I spent quite a period wandering about the historic places, including the so-called Wailing Wall.

The most enjoyable part of the whole holiday was an organised donkey ride around the Mount of Olives.

Just as we were on the finishing stretch I was informed by one of the guides of the correct procedure to be adopted to increase the effective speed of the donkey.

The idea seems to be to put your hand behind you on the part of the donkey's back which is maintained by the saddle movement, and coolly squeeze until he begins to show signs of more movement.

Well I finished the last mile so just like Cowboy Charlie. The thing was bucking like hell and I've rarely had such an exhilarating time. I'm determined to take up the equestrian art as soon as possible because I am sure I'd prefer it even to cycling.

Well I was very sorry when my time was up and I had to catch my train as per a very definite instruction by the R.T.O. [Railway Transport Officer]

So many people go there for leave, the train space is scarce. Well it did me a lump of good. If I'm lucky I might wangle some more.

My few days in Palestine were leave, and a good leave too....

Jack's working conditions were not pleasant. One of the places he worked was in the caves at Tura-el-Asman, in the Mokkatan hills south of Cairo. Interestingly these caves were excavated by the ancient Egyptians when limestone was required for encasing the pyramids. They were used as maintenance units for aircraft and engine repairs. There was also a small hospital.

Jack's letter of 22 February 1944 details his regime:

06:15 hours it's bloody cold usually 10° when little Chico [his servant] brings a cup of something supposed to resemble tea.

This enables me to gain enough willpower to scramble out of bed into PT Kit and quarter mile run to the parade sand, where I, repeat, I take the officers and sergeants in PT, and finish at 7. Washed and breakfast by 7.30 and on the gharry [horse - drawn cab] up to the caves. 2 mile walk, if you miss the wagon, all uphill.

In the morning there is always a sandstorm, which never really stops in this part of the world.

Anyway 7.30 to 12.30 we are in the caves

working with no fresh air or natural light. There is a 10 minute break for tea usually 12.30 to 13.15 down on the gharry and back for Tiffin. 13.15 to 17.30 work with no break again in caves leaving everybody completely tired and dissipated

On 21 March 1945 he writes despondently:

Very soon now the Middle East will be nothing more than a vast transit camp, with myself and many others trapped here for a period.

And then, suddenly, the war ends, but for Jack without a bang.

VE Day, 8 May 1945 came and went, but Jack's time in the Middle Eastern Theatre drags on...

21/5

As you may have guessed I have been moving around with a capital M. I started from my old unit with a pile of ridiculous equipment meant for certain operational purpose. After hawking it for hundreds of miles, I finally arrived back in Egypt though too late for any celebration.

I feel that that was a fitting anti-climax to my war effort. Without any great desire for beer et cetera I did not miss the booze-ups that seem to have ensued. All I want to do just now is get back into civvies, and see everybody again. The mere fact that the war in Europe has ended doesn't affect me in the least. It's much better to

256

feel now that Hitler's V monstrosities[15] have finished, and that all the people I hold dear are still safe.

The days drag on.

Just now I'm living in a billet reasonably near Cairo. I have very little to grumble about, except of course we have just had a flood.

You know I must be getting infinitely blasé these days. There were dead bodies of various animals including a horse washed past my front door a few hours ago and I couldn't even raise interest. Maybe it's because I'm nervously tired or something. Anyhow, luckily we managed to get a respectable billet which is clean, immune from floodwaters, but lots of natives have been drowned locally. The railroad was wrecked and the disaster was enormous, but it just doesn't interest me any more.

I want to go home.

In the last letter we have, written on 6 June 1945, Jack writes:

A piece of news in that I received the opportunity to tell a very important person just how much I have been messed around in the last two years. He was surprised to see that I was still a Flight Sergeant after nearly three years. He assured me something would be done so

---

15 V1 flying bombs and V2 rockets

expect the best.

And then, maybe more importantly he tells Dally,

Please, darling don't let me panic you into
telling anybody as yet, but I feel that as a result
of my chat with a friend as (page 1), I may be
returning home in the not very distant future.
As there is a possibility, I feel you should know.

Please don't raise anybody's false hopes by
telling them, but my judgement indicates that
you may rely on it.

Jack's time in Egypt came to an end in June 1945.
He returned to London, and the letters stopped.

He married Dally on March 3rd the following
year.

Chapter Fifteen: Jack and Dally emigrate

My mother said it was the first big Jewish wedding since the war ended. It was on 3 March 1946 at Stoke Newington Synagogue. The reception, dinner and dance was at Shoreditch Town Hall, and by all accounts it was a humdinger! The bride was exquisite, as the photographs testify. My mother wore her long black hair beautifully coiffed and wearing an exquisite white silk satin dress with a long train. Jack was in the customary black dinner suit, looking very spruce. There were bridesmaids, flower girls and pageboys.

Jack and Dell's wedding which took place on 3 March 1946. The wedding ceremony took place at Stoke Newington Synagogue, Shacklewell Lane. The reception was at Shoreditch Town Hall.

As I write this, I think that there were so many

ways either one could have been injured or killed. Dally was in London for much of the Blitz (despite Jack's pleas to move out). Five houses in her parents' street (Teesdale Street) were obliterated with many fatalities. Even their own house, 39 Teesdale Street was severely damaged by a bomb.

Dally hated going to the shelters. Once she cried to her mother, "I woke up with a tramp's toes in my face!". Her mother answered prophetically, "Never mind, one day you will be a princess."

My mother's response said, "And I was!"

Their later life in South Africa was extremely luxurious compared to their lives in Britain. Postwar Britain was not a happy place. There were still severe shortages. The winter of 1947 saw the heaviest snowfall since the nineteenth century. The freeze lasted from mid-January till mid-March.

Dell and Jack in 1947

Jack was thinking of his past, and their future. I

think of the ways my father could have met a very different fate: lashing huge aerials in gales and blizzards, climbing 350ft masts in equally inclement weather. There was the horror of Dieppe, when he could have been killed by a German bullet, an intended one from his own side, or the grenades he had strapped to his person as an insurance; and there were his acute cases of malaria... Jack and Dally were indeed fortunate, not only to have survived, but to have all their close family survive the blitz as well.

We were quite amazed, recently, to find a postcard from Pourville, written in August 1947. My father went back on the fifth anniversary of the Dieppe Raid; I don't remember him mentioning this return visit. There was a ceremony to commemorate the lives lost. Over three thousand Canadians had been killed, wounded or taken prisoner.

It must have been a deeply moving experience returning to the village where he had experienced so much carnage.

Immediately after the war Jack was offered a post at RAF College Cranwell. It was there that he was advised to change his name in case any of the enemy with long memories wanted to make reprisals. He left the RAF and started civilian life. Nissenthall became Nissen.

Dally and Jack had been allocated a much sought-after, semi-detached house, on which they put a down payment. It was at 3 Carnarvon Drive, Hayes. Jack had a small radio repair shop nearby on Bourne Circus, Hayes, but still worked at EMI/HMV Hayes setting up television set production. The shop struggled, and the last straw was when a horse and cart went past. The horse kicked a stone breaking the plate glass window. This was a blow for the young couple. They were insured, but the insurance company called it an "Act of God" and would not pay up.

The Jan Smuts government in South Africa were seeking radar engineers. Prime Minister Smuts had visited Jack's radar station at Bolt Head during the Second World War. Jack was promised a fine job with prospects of promotion, in a glorious climate and a new life. It is scandalous that Radar boffins who were largely responsible for the success of the Battle of Britain, and the D Day landings, were barred from marching in the Victory Parades. The brain drain was starting. British scientists felt under-valued, and were moving to other countries.

In *Britain's Shield; Radar and the Defeat of the Luftwaffe* published by Amberley Publishing, David Zimmerman writes:

> Watson-Watt and several other of his former Bawdsey staff chafed at the lack of recognition. Not one radar scientist was invited to participate in the victory parade.....

> Watson-Watt was right to feel unappreciated after 1945, since he and his team achieved one of the most remarkable scientific and technological accomplishments of the 20th century. They provided Britain with a shield of radar which allowed Fighter Command to defeat the Luftwaffe. This enabled Britain to survive and, arguably, saved western liberal democracy.

Jack was probably feeling under-valued too, and

here was an opportunity he could not afford to miss. He hankered after a better life in the sun, and the young couple decided in 1948 to hand the house in Hayes over to my mother's brother Max and my father's sister Marie, who now had a little girl, my cousin Adrienne. My mother was very loath to leave her lovely family. (She adored them all, especially Adrienne.) But Jack had made up his mind.

Jack with Cliff Robinson and another radar friend on the boat to South Africa in 1948.

My father went out first, and my plucky mother, (now known as Dell), pregnant with me, travelled to Cape Town on an uncomfortable *Carnarvon Castle*. It had not yet been converted back from its role as a troopship during the war.

Still she had her lovely husband and a grand future waiting for her. What could go wrong? They were both looking forward to a good life in the south: sunny weather, spacious accommodation and a well-paid job in the South African Air Force. Jack had been invited to erect up-to-date radar defences around South Africa. They had a golden future ahead of them. Coming from post war, food-rationed Britain, it could only be good.

Jack had fallen in love with South Africa, when his ship had stopped off at Durban in the war, on his way to Egypt.

On 26 May 1948 there was a catastrophic (for them) election. The Nationalists led by Dr Malan, a Dutch Reform Cleric, beat Jan Smuts' United Party and so began the white Afrikanerisation of the country. The Minister of Defence, Frans Christaan Erasmus, wanted to purge the forces of anything English.

In the Air Force it was a must to speak Afrikaans. Newly arrived English Jack was told it was a pre-requisite for his job. Undaunted, and knowing German, Jack learned Afrikaans in three weeks.

They gave him an exam, which he passed. They were non-plussed, so gave him a supplementary exam, asking "the bones of the hand" in Afrikaans. They were determined he should not pass the second exam. He didn't know them (even in English), so he failed.

He was allowed to remain in the SAAF (South African Air Force), but the golden job disappeared, my pregnant mother had arrived, and so he was forced to take their offer of the lowest rank in the Air Force and, therefore, the lowest pay.

There was no question of them coming back to England; even if they had wanted to, he had no means of buying himself out of the three-year contract, or getting the return fare.

Life was hard. They were transferred to Pretoria. When I was born in the Arcadia Nursing Home, Pretoria, the nurses did not hide their antipathy for my

English mother. On the other hand, my parents told me their very kind Afrikaans next door neighbour took pity on them, and built a kitchen table for them out of orange boxes.

I really did have a drawer as my crib when I was born!

The Jewish community, however, soon took them under their wing.

Even before I was born, in November 1948, Lena and Shalom Lazar (who became their adopted parents, and adopted grandparents of my brother and me) took them to the Governor General's Garden party. (Lena acquired a large dress for my mother to wear.) We have photos of them in the garden. My mother and Auntie Lena resplendent in fancy hats and surrounded by the beautiful garden flowers. In 1952 my brother Paul was born. He still lives in South Africa.

As soon as Jack's three-year contract was up, Jack left the Air Force and opened up a radio repair shop.

The treatment of my father became a cause célèbre. It was later brought up in the South African Parliament on 23 May 1951 and made the newspapers. We have a copy of South African Hansard. There was a long exchange between the Minster for Defence, FC Erasmus, and opposition MP Russell. Russell stated:

> I mentioned it on account of the fact that the Minister has said that he is satisfied that radar throughout the country is being brought satisfactorily up-to-date. We know otherwise from reports, which the Minister has not denied, of a Mr Nissen, who was described as the finest instrument maker in the Southern Hemisphere and who, unfortunately for us, has

left the force.

It even made headlines in the Johannesburg Star April 9, 1951.

Radar expert from England kept as private in SAAF. Bilingual policy forcing more technicians to leave as contracts end

The government would rather have an Afrikaner-pure Air Force than strong Radar defence.

Dell and the author outside the shop at 33 Bureau Lane, Pretoria.

Jack's shop was extremely popular. He had time for everyone. He encouraged young people's interest in electronics, and seems to have carried on the informing and teaching, just the way that Alan Blumlein encouraged him. Adam Farson who later had a successful career in electronics writes (in February 2020) from Vancouver.

I first had occasion to visit your father's shop in Bureau Lane when I discovered a US-made Webster wire recording machine at my father's office, and learned that your dad was a Webster dealer. I recall that he was even kind enough to lend me a machine to take home and play with one weekend. I was all of 11 years old at the time. Your Dad and I got on famously because he had a tremendous amount of knowledge which he was willing to share with me, a most willing student. I used to "drop in" at the shop quite frequently of a Saturday (the only day I had off school and was able to go to the city centre) and spend an hour or so chatting with your father. The knowledge I gained from him was certainly one of the building-blocks of my subsequent career.

Among other things, Jack taught me about the different types of microphones and their characteristics, and helped me construct an electronic audio-level meter which I then connected to our radio set at home. He also provided me with most of the parts needed for this project.

Of course, the Official Secrets Act being what it was, the subject of your father's wartime work never came up. I became aware of it only many years afterwards.

When High Fidelity came in, Jack continued with

the repairs, but then began making custom-built HiFi units and eventually stereo sets. Norman Dawson met my father in the shop and began working part time for him. He was a highly skilled carpenter. He made cabinets for HiFi's and stereos. Sometimes he would adapt antique furniture when a particular customer wanted the HiFi or Stereo concealed. Later Norma, Norman's wife, joined and became a much-valued shop assistant and lifelong friend. Jack's work was extremely sought after and, of course, everyone loved his warm, gentle modest manner.

Another young man who my father mentored was Savas Couvaras. He writes in June 2020:

> I first met Mr Nissen one afternoon when I went to their home to collect my sister who was varsity friends with Linda, Mr Nissen's daughter. While waiting for my sister I was invited in for tea and got to know the Nissens and I heard the first-hand stories of his active involvement during the war.
>
> As a youngster I always was interested in electronics such as building crystal sets et cetera. But after becoming friendly and with Mr Nissen's advice and assistance I was able to build my first audio amplifier which I still have some 60 odd years later.
>
> The Nissens had a shop in Bureau Lane in Pretoria which sold records and electrical items in the front and with his workshop at the back. My sister and I would buy the latest hit parade records at special prices and I would purchase parts to build my amp. Jack Nissen played an

important part in my introduction to electronics such as walkie-talkies and other novel items which were only seen in the movies in those days. Electronics is still my hobby and I would've loved his input on satellite technology especially in tracing various footprints and decoding the signals. A friendly person always smiling and always ready to give assistance and advice to anyone.

The shops increased in size, with a record shop, run by my mother in the front, and a workshop behind. Their by-line was "Listen with Nissen". Jack trained members of the black community in electronics to help with the workload. Harold (who later worked in the workshop) once told me that training black people to acquire superior skills was frowned upon by the authorities, and that if a stranger walked into the back workroom, the workers would leave the bench, and grab brooms, as if they were cleaners. I don't remember this, but I do remember Vivian, Sam and others at the work bench. The record shop flourished with my mother and Norma welcoming all and sundry. The loud music could be heard up and down Bureau Lane. Quite often a little impromptu "dance party" broke out. From Tchaikovsky to the Beatles, everyone in the area knew what was playing at Jack Nissen's. Customers were also treated to cups of tea and sandwiches from the shop around the corner. It really was a very happy place.

My grandmother, Jack's mother Annie, came out from England in the early fifties, with her son Harold, to live in Pretoria. Harold looked on Jack as a proxy father (he was twenty years older). Harold's barmitzvah was held in the Old Synagogue, in Paul Kruger Street. I distinctly remember Harold having his head covered with a prayer shawl (tallit) and I wondering (at age 4) whether his head would ever appear again. The Old Synagogue was then closed, and the more modern orthodox synagogue was built in Pretorius Street. Sadly, the now defunct Old Synagogue later became the courthouse for the infamous apartheid trials. Nelson Mandela was tried there.

Harold eventually emigrated to Canada where he married the lovely Arlene and had three fine children of his own, Alan, Michael and Rhonda.

As we became more affluent, after renting flats (Orpheum Mansions, downtown Pretoria: Treverton Court in leafy Sunnyside) and houses, in Prospect Street and Hilda Street, we eventually moved into a lovely home of our own with a large garden at 359 Nicolson Street, Brooklyn. My brother Paul's happy memory of this period in the early sixties is of our father coming home from work, and taking him to Hillcrest Swimming Baths every summer afternoon. This was their "special" time together. It is so good that our father found time to do this, even after a tiring day's work.

*Jack and Paul, the author's brother, on the beach at Durban
1955*

Every year we had our annual holiday in Durban.
The Jeremy Taylor song Ag Pleez Deddy could have
been written about us. We would pile into the car in
Pretoria and make the eight- or nine-hour trek to
Durban. The holiday started when we climbed in the

car, and we could barely contain our excitement. Most days we would breakfast in the hotel and then cross the Marine Parade to the North or South beach. My dad was brilliant at making huge (to us) sand castles and digging deep holes. He especially loved the surf and we would take it in turns on the lilo to come surfing in on our stomachs. We picnicked on the beach and in the afternoon would go for drives to places like Zululand and the beautiful Valley of a Thousand Hills. He often talked about stopping in Durban on the way to Egypt. He had dreamed of returning, and so he did, for many years.

Each summer Sunday we would go to the Jewish Wingate Country Club which was heaven for all of us. Jews were not welcome in the other clubs. Wingate was set in acres of lovely grounds with a beautifully landscaped golf course, bowling green, tennis courts and an indoor restaurant where we would all sit down on a very hot summer Christmas day to eat roast stuffed turkey and Christmas pudding. Health and Safety did not seem to matter then, as we examined each mouthful with our tongues to see if we had been dished a silver "tickey" (threepenny bit).

Our particular domain at Wingate, for all the summer, was the large pool where we would spend hours splashing about and doing "tricks". One trick for was me to climb onto my dad's shoulders in the shallow end, get my balance, stand erect and while he walked underwater to the deep end (he could still hold his breath for a long time!) I looked like I was walking on water. The poolside open air restaurant was our favourite eating place, with quite delicious steak sandwiches and Kola tonic drinks. (Jack's favourite non-alcoholic tipple, as he never enjoyed alcohol).

After a while, a swimming pool was built in our own back garden, and we stopped going to Wingate. In Nicolson Street, we all spent idyllic summer Sundays by the pool, with Jack barbecuing in his swimming shorts, and my mother, assisted by the maid, Bella, creating delicious salads and desserts. My mother loved entertaining in this manner, and we were very happy to receive guests. Every Sunday morning Cyril Freedman would come, sometimes with his son Brian. Later on Brian was at Pretoria University with me and he also emigrated to England. We remained close friends until his very premature death in 2017.

Cyril was also from London, so he and my parents would spend hours talking about the "heim" (Yiddish word for home) and how fortunate they were not to be there under grey rainy skies and cold. The garden and pool in the summer were the centre of our life. Jack encouraged us to swim underwater, so passing on a skill, that had saved his life at Dieppe. He was a very happy, modest, popular man, and a gentle loving, witty father.

All the while we were living in a bubble. We rarely came across Anti-Semitism, but the English were not popular with the Afrikaners. My father was. He had friends of every race, creed and colour, and from every walk of life. But he was well aware how some Afrikaners had made his life extremely difficult.

Going back to when I was four. I asked, "Is Dr Malan, (our then prime minister) a doctor who makes you better?"

He answered "No, he is a doctor who makes you sick!"

I remember trying to make sense of this in my childish way, and came to the conclusion that there were doctors who went round making you sick, so that other doctors could come and make you better!

After the Sharpeville massacre in 1960, in which about seventy unarmed protesters were killed, my father and mother began talking about emigrating to America. They had a great friend, Major Cruciana, an Air Attaché at the American Embassy. He suggested La Jolla near San Diego in California, and I think it nearly happened, except that fate intervened, when my father read a condensed book in the Reader's Digest. It was the long reach of Dieppe, that changed their lives.

Chapter Sixteen: The Quentin Reynolds affair

The Readers Digest condensed book was *My Life In Court* by Louis Nizer.

In it Nizer talked about a libel case his client Quentin Reynolds pursued against a fellow journalist, Pegler. I include below an excerpt from *Green Beach* by James Leasor. James Leasor wrote *Green Beach* (the story of the Dieppe Raid) with my father in 1975. The two became good friends and I am still in touch with his son Stuart.

In the 1950s, a curious legal footnote was written to the story of Jack's mission. Quentin Reynolds, the American journalist whose BBC broadcasts when America was still neutral had done so much to raise British morale, had been aboard HMS Calpe during the Dieppe Raid[16]. He had learned of Jack's involvement, but, of course, not knowing his name he had given him a nickname 'Professor Wendell'. In 1955, another American journalist, Westbrook Pegler, who wrote a column syndicated in 186 newspapers, branded Reynolds a liar, a braggart, and a cowardly absentee war correspondent. [This was the time of McCarthyism and Reynolds was a liberal journalist and war correspondent who went on the Dieppe Raid]. Not surprisingly, Reynolds sued him. The case dragged on inconclusively until Pegler's Counsel asked about Professor

---

16 Quentin Reynolds wrote about this in *Dress Rehearsal* published in 1943

Wendell. He demanded that Reynolds should admit that the story of the mad scientist who went on the Dieppe raid was a 'quirk of your mind, a falsification of your own vivid imagination…

"If there was such a man, give the court his name. If you can't give the name, admit that it was a story that you read in Superman comics, Space Cadet, or Mr Batman… What person in his normal senses would invade enemy occupied territory with his body lined up in the sights of his friends behind, and the Germans before him, both with their fingers on their triggers? I demand that you now give the name of the man or admit here and now that you are a liar."

Quentin Reynolds was confounded, for he did not know Jack's real name. Yet if he could not discover it, he could lose the whole case on this point.

A former member of Lord Mountbatten's staff, Colonel Jock Lawrence, happened to be in New York, and he read a report of this case in a newspaper, and he willingly testified as to what Jack had done. Pegler's Council demanded that he give Jack's name in open court. Lawrence refused, although he knew it, because Combined Operations had never released the name. Instead, he wrote it down and handed it to the judge. As a result, Reynolds won his case and $175,001 [the largest award in any libel case, up to then] punitive damages against Pegler and the newspapers that employed him.

It is quite striking how the Quentin Reynolds thread, first visible in Chapter 2, when he serendipitously offers Jack and John Strong a lift to London runs through my father's biography from then on.

Considering Jack's role was "Top Secret", it is strange that Quentin Reynolds was told so much about the brilliant civilian scientist who was accompanied by men from his own side, and whose task it was to ensure this radar genius did not fall into enemy hands.

Interestingly while he was in Egypt, in October 1943, Dally sent Jack a copy of Quentin Reynold's Dress Rehearsal, and it even passed the censor! There are a few inaccuracies such as the number of men in the bodyguard, but it is obviously about Jack.

Jack talks about the book in an obscure way, but from the fact that she sent it, and him commenting on it, we can be sure Dally knew exactly who Professor Wendell was.

November 9 1943

That book has turned up and I've managed to read the more interesting parts.

Incidentally Quentin Reynolds has written a book on that show in August last year. In it he refers to a mysterious person by the name of "Professor Wendle" [sic].

He goes to great lengths to describe him as a wizard bloke in every way, that of course real names in that particular case cannot be mentioned.

As you know he was not killed, but I agree with

him when he says that it's a good job the professor managed to get away. Even if he didn't have any trousers left. That's a story you don't know. [Jack lost most of his clothing in the swim to the landing craft].

Quentin Reynolds speculated about a civilian scientist who had gone on the Dieppe Raid. Of course Jack was not a civilian, and his bodyguard comprised ten men, and not four. The book was published in 1943, only one year after the Dieppe Raid. In the preface he introduces Jack:

> There is even some fiction in the following pages. Not much – but some. This book was submitted to Mountbatten's office for censorship. I could not use the real name of the radio genius who was to be shot by his own troops, rather than be captured. So I invented the name "Wendell" for him.
>
> I stood there on the bridge, gazing at the scene ahead… Pourville lay about halfway between Dieppe and Varangeville. The South Saskatchewan regiment was to land there and flank the high ramp which began one mile to the right of Dieppe, and stretched the mile and quarter to Pourville. In the back of the ramp and about half a mile to the left of Pourville, the aerial photographs showed that a radio detection finder was located. This was to be destroyed or, if possible, dismantled and brought back by the South Saskatchewan regiment or by the Queens Own Cameron Highlanders who were to follow them. A

civilian was to accompany the South Saskatchewan lads - A very important civilian. He was Professor "Wendell" and Professor "Wendell's" real name is known to very few people in Britain. Actually, he is the developer of new stunts in radio location. He is responsible for the immense improvement in this new branch of defensive warfare, and it is due to him that the RAF and anti-aircraft groups in Britain are always able to spot the Germans long before they arrive at their objectives.

Professor "Wendell" had a bodyguard of four soldiers whose only job was to stay close to him from the time they landed on the beach in front of Pourville. They were to ignore the Germans, and keep their eyes on the professor. They were to keep not only their eyes but their drawn guns on the professor. The professor was to look over the German radio detection finder located just behind the wall to find out if there was anything new about it. With his immense technical experience in this sort of thing, a few minutes alone with it should suffice. But suppose the Germans proved to be too strong? Suppose they surprised the professor and at least four bodyguards with the drawn guns? The answer was simple. The four soldiers had orders to shoot the Professor immediately. Britain could not afford to have this genius of radio location fall into enemy hands. The drug [supposed truth drug] which sounds as though it came out of a comic strip was no joke to Mountbatten and his aides. They knew that no man alive had the willpower to combat the influence of a drug that had just one property - it makes you tell the truth. Far better to kill "Wendell" than to have him fall into the hands of the Germans, who would make him reveal the secrets that have made the British radio finders the best in the world. "Wendell" knew the great risk he ran. His sense of patriotism and his scientific curiosity as to what the Germans might have in the way of something new, I am sure, conquered any feeling of fear he might have entertained.

The office of Combined Operations will neither confirm nor deny the presence of Professor "Wendell" on the raid. However, I know the story to be true and I know that it was his own idea that he be killed rather than fall into German hands. Fortunately for him and for us, he escaped after accomplishing his task.

I remember, one night when a lot of us were sitting around the Savoy. An alert had been sounded and it seemed silly to go to bed. After nearly a year's freedom from air raids in London, we didn't quite know how to take them in our stride any more. We sat around waiting for what might develop. I was with Larry Rue of the *Chicago Tribune*, Ned Russell of the *UP*, Red Mueller of *Newsweek*, Eric Baume of an Australian syndicate, Aneurin Bevin the Labor [sic] M.P., and a few others. When raiders are overhead, you argue about silly things. It happened at a time when most of us were broke and someone inevitably asked 'How could any of us make a million dollars quickly?' Each one of us had what seemed to be a perfectly reasonable suggestion…Then one more practical-minded than the rest of us said "Capture Professor "Wendell" and get him to Germany. Goering would give a million in cash on the line just to have him, so he could feed him some of the truth serum and learn about the British methods of locating approaching planes and ships."

That won the prize, because we all knew that the Germans would pay anything to have the Professor with them. He would be assured of kindly treatment – oh, such kindly treatment. Nothing would happen to him as long as the whole scientific fund of information lodged in his professorial mind was not exhausted.

Anyhow, this is the civilian who was to accompany the South Saskatchewan on the flank movement; it was not a very pleasant assignment.

On reading the article in the Reader's Digest, my father contacted Quentin Reynolds.
This is his reply:

January 5, 1962

Dear Jack Nissenthall,

It was exciting to receive your kind letter which was forwarded through to me by Reader's Digest. I certainly wish you had been in New York during my trial. Pegler's attorney made a big thing of my reference to Dr Wendell. He really thought I had been writing fiction. He asked me where I'd heard the story, and I told him quite honestly that Lord Mountbatten had given it to me. I added that Mountbatten told me that no one except upper echelon Combined Operations men knew your real name, but that I could use the story if I called you Dr Wendell. I don't think the jury believed me (it was a rather cloak and dagger tale), but happily, Colonel Jock Lawrence of Mountbatten's press relations staff at the time was in New York and he testified as to the accuracy of the story. Pegler's lawyer insisted that Jock give your real name. He knew it but said that as far as he knew Combined Operations had not as yet released it. He added, however that he would write your name out and give it to the judge. He did so, and the jury was so impressed with his testimony that it believed him. So even though you were several thousand miles away from the courtroom you did help me a great deal.

The possibility of my ever getting to your part of the world is remote but if I ever do, I will give you fair warning.

Very sincerely

Quentin Reynolds

Even though the Raid was still covered by the Official Secrets Act, spurred on by Quentin Reynolds, Jack wrote *The Wizard War* a comprehensive account of his involvement with radar and his war years, up to and including the Dieppe Raid. I have included that material in the previous chapters. Jack did as Quentin Reynolds suggested and wrote from South Africa in 1963 to R V Jones and other radar people. This is R V Jones two page reply.

MINISTRY OF DEFENCE,

LONDON, S.W.1.

16th October 1963

Dear Nissen

Thank you very much for your letter of 2nd October. I, of course, remember you very well and have often thought about your part in the Dieppe raid.

Your memory about the information that we extracted from the radar plots is quite correct. We obtained a very good insight into the workings of the German radar system. They were not particularly spectacular in speed of plotting or in raid handling capacity; indeed, their operational capacity was for a long time not nearly as good as ours – where they excelled was in the accuracy of plotting. I am not sure how much security grading there is attached to the knowledge of our use of those radar plots, but I think that I have seen them mentioned in one of the official histories.

As regards the Dieppe raid itself, one interesting thing that did result was that we lost some early models of the Churchill tank. These were tested by the Germans, and fortunately we were able to get hold of the German test report so that we were able to rectify the weak points which the Germans had found. You can certainly mention my name to your brothers if it will help at all.

About two years after the raid, just around D-Day, I met a Canadian major who told me he thought I was dead. This was because, he said, he thought that I myself had gone on the Dieppe raid and he had detailed two men to shoot me if I was in danger of

being/

J. Nissen, Esq.

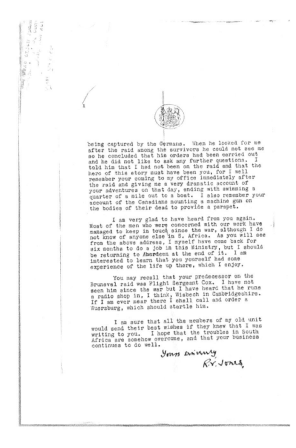

being captured by the Germans. When he looked for me after the raid among the survivors he could not see me so he concluded that his orders had been carried out and he did not like to ask any further questions. I told him that I had not been on the raid and that the hero of this story must have been you, for I well remember your coming to my office immediately after the raid and giving me a very dramatic account of your adventures on that day, ending with swimming a quarter of a mile out to a boat. I also remember your account of the Canadians mounting a machine gun on the bodies of their dead to provide a parapet.

I am very glad to have heard from you again. Most of the men who were concerned with our work have managed to keep in touch since the war, although I do not know of anyone else in S. Africa. As you will see from the above address, I myself have come back for six months to do a job in this Ministry, but I should be returning to Aberdeen at the end of it. I am interested to learn that you yourself had some experience of the life up there, which I enjoy.

You may recall that your predecessor on the Bruneval raid was Flight Sergeant Cox. I have not seen him since the war but I have heard that he runs a radio shop in, I think, Wisbech in Cambridgeshire. If I am ever near there I shall call and order a Wuerzburg, which should startle him.

I am sure that all the members of my old unit would send their best wishes if they knew that I was writing to you. I hope that the troubles in South Africa are somehow overcome, and that your business continues to do well.

Yours sincerely,

R.V. Jones,

In 1975, the book *Green Beach* was written by James Leasor. The British film producer, Michael Klinger had read Jack's story in the Observer in 1967. He approached Jack with a view to making a movie of the amazing Dieppe story. He introduced Jack to the author James Leasor and they were very keen for the book to be written and the story to be screened. Sadly nothing came of the movie, although we are very grateful to James Leasor for the excellent rendering of Jack's story in *Green Beach* which was a best seller worldwide, published by Heinemann, and translated into fifteen languages.

James Leasor and Jack went to Canada and found the man, who had swum out with Jack to the landing craft, Roy Hawkins.

James Leasor writes:

When Jack Nissen and I first arrived in Ottawa, we went to see Gordon Way, the chief public relations officer of the Department for Veterans Affairs – a most efficient Canadian ministry that exists simply to safeguard the interests of all who have served Canada in the armed forces. We explained to Mr Way that we sought his assistance in tracing some of the members of the South Saskatchewan Regiment who had landed at Pourville on August 19, 1942. Mr Way replied that he had received a number of requests for help from other writers who had reconstructed the story of the Dieppe Raid over the years, and he personally wondered what new material could now be found after all this time.

'There is only one thing I would like to know about that campaign,' he went on, 'A British scientist landed with the Canadians with orders that he must be shot rather than captured. Now, that would make an interesting story. I have always wondered what happened to him….'

Lord Mountbatten appreciated the importance of the Freya [German Radar] as one of Jubilee's

16 targets, [Operation Jubilee/the Dieppe Raid] but he had no idea of the incredible conditions which Jack Nissenthall willingly accepted when he agreed to try and learn its secrets. When I showed Lord Mountbatten the manuscript of this book, he commented, "If I had been aware of the orders given to the escort to shoot him rather than letting him be captured, I would immediately have cancelled them."

While Lord Mountbatten had been responsible for the top-level planning of Dieppe, and had approved the proposal to extract all possible information about the Freya, the detailed arrangements for this operation were left to the Army commander and the Air Force commander, while the Air Ministry produced the radar expert. Lord Mountbatten had therefore no idea - and there was no reason why he should - that Nissenthall was also to attempt to enter the radar station. Because the defences around all German radio stations had been heavily increased after Bruneval, this would have seemed to him an impossible task – as indeed it proved.

'It was my impression that he was going to cut the landline wires so as to force the station to go off air, which worked well.' Lord Mountbatten recalled. 'I am horrified to learn that a man was chosen who knew about the cavity magnetron, and put in a position where he might have been tortured to the point of giving away the secret, and so it was arranged for ten men to shoot him so he would not be captured.'

What concerned Lord Mountbatten particularly was the fact that while Combined Operations maintained an organisation for the purpose of providing former German Jews enlisted in the commandos, and selected for particularly hazardous assignment with completely false identities, even to letters, backgrounds and relations, no use whatever was made of these sophisticated facilities on Jack Nissenthall's behalf. He could easily have been given a complete Canadian identity, but this was never requested.

'Never at any time have I heard of sending people out with instructions to kill one of their own men. Another failure of the machine below me was that nobody told me afterwards that Nissenthall had returned safely. If I'd been told, he would most certainly have been decorated on the spot. To get him to do what he did and give him nothing is churlish.'

Chapter Seventeen: Move to Canada

In 1977 Jack and Dell emigrated to Canada. They had a very happy life in Toronto. They spent part of the winters in Florida, to avoid the extreme cold. It was a good choice for two reasons. Jack was honoured in Canada for his part in the Dieppe Raid, for which operation the bulk of the servicemen were Canadian, and he was offered Canadian citizenship while on his tour around Canada with James Leasor.

Also, his two brothers Michael and Harold had emigrated to Canada.

Mickey had died in 1975, but his wife Myrtle and their daughter Karen were still in Canada, as were Harold, his wife Arlene, and their three children, Alan, Michael and Rhonda.

Early on in Jack's life in Canada, he attended a lecture at the Ontario Science Centre, Toronto with his brother Harold who was an audio-visual engineer.

The lecture was presented by Brian Parrott, Manager of Electronics at the Science Centre and afterwards Jack was introduced to him.

Brian and Jack became buddies. Brian was a pilot and flew Jack around in his Cessna 150. Brian wrote in 2020, "I flew Jack to many places in Southern Ontario. One of his favourite places was Hamilton airport to visit the Canadian Warplane Heritage Museum where they had many WW2 aircraft including a Lancaster."

In Canada Jack was a popular speaker and invited to talk at many Veteran and Radar organisations. He was also a guest speaker at US Ranger events, having befriended survivors of the fifty US Rangers who attended the Dieppe raid reunions. These were the first American soldiers to fight in Europe during the Second World War.

One exciting event of which my father spoke with enthusiasm, was a visit in May 1993 to the top-secret NORAD (North American Air Defence Command) complex, 680 feet underground; three storeys tall; can house over 400 people under a lake at North Bay, north-eastern Ontario. Jack, who was well-known in Canada as a war hero for his involvement in the Dieppe Raid, was invited to speak at a mess dinner of 22 Wing.

We have a letter of thanks from Colonel Ewen Cornick in which he asks Jack "to accept my sincere gratitude for the visit of yourself and Mr Parrott to 22 Wing and for speaking at our Mess Dinner. You must justifiably take great pride in your tremendous contributions leading to this generation of radar sensor."

He later adds, "I know that I personally enjoyed our discussions of early radar development and your fascinating wartime experiences."

Of course for my father it was a great honour to be shown the cutting-edge radar technology, which was being utilised in this highly complex nuclear bunker.

Jack, who was well-known in Canada as a war hero for his involvement in the Dieppe Raid, was invited to speak at a mess dinner of 22 Wing in May 1993 at the top-secret NORAD (North American Air Defence Command) complex. He is pictured here with Brian Parrott and Colonel E R Cornick.

Presented To

MR. JACK NISSEN
ALIAS "Professor Wendell"
Guest Speaker
22 WING MESS DINNER
6 May 1993

---

22 Wing
Hornell Heights, ON
P0H 1P0

22e Escadre
Hornell Heights (ON)
P0H 1P0

From Colonel E.R. Cornick, OMM, CD

25 May 1993

Dear Jack,

Please accept my sincere gratitude for the visit of yourself and Mr Parrot to 22 Wing and for speaking at our Mess Dinner. I certainly hope that you found your stay pleasant and your trip to the FPS 124 Short Range Development radar site interesting. You must justifiably take great pride in your tremendous contributions leading to this generation of radar sensor.

Your time spent here at North Bay was most productive, and, I feel, very stimulating for those fortunate enough to have spent some time with you. I know that I personally enjoyed our discussions of early radar development and your fascinating wartime experiences. I am, however, not unexpectedly reminded by many that a single after-dinner discussion has only just whet our appetites for these topics.

I look forward, as we discussed after dinner, to your next visit and the opportunity to pick up where we left off. In anticipation of that occasion, I am now being fitted for a brand new pair of contact lenses which I believe will come in handy. Will you keep my secret?

Please pass along my best regards to Mr Parrot and, once again, my sincere thanks to you both.

Yours truly,

Ewen

Mr Jack Nissen
191 Eglinton Avenue East
Suite 301
Toronto, ON
M4P 1K1

P.S. Have included copy of the to your published, & several photos. Thanks again

NORAD plaque and letter of thanks

291

Jack in front of a FW190 at the Canadian Warplane Heritage
Museum at Hamilton airport where they had many WW2
aircraft including a Lancaster bomber.

Director-General of the Science Centre, Tuzo Wilson an eminent geophysicist and geologist was introduced to Jack by Brian. On meeting Jack, it wasn't long before he mentioned two display machines that weren't functioning properly. He asked if Jack, with his knowledge of electronics, could take them home and solve the problem.

This Jack did, and so began his final career. He formed a company *Museum Electronics*. Over a ten-year period, he trained 40 subcontractors to produce exhibits; working in conjunction with the Ontario Science Centre he designed and built all the exhibits for the Palace of Science, Beijing, the Travelling Science Circus, in Nagasaki, Japan and the Museo de los Niños, Caracas. His machines were on display at the World Trade Fair, Brisbane, The Science Museum, South Kensington, Smithsonian and Museum of Cinematography, Bradford, UK.

Dr Doron Swade MBE head of AVEC (Audio-visual, Electronic, and Computer-based Displays) at the Science Museum, London wrote to me in February 2020:

My main impressions are of the sense I had of him overall - humour, warmth, understanding, integrity, great independence of thought and insight, all from a standpoint outside cliche and received thinking.

In a subsequent email Doron writes:

At the time that Jack was active in museum electronics, working exhibits in museums had a bad reputation for being dismally unreliable.

Museum marketing departments dreaded complaints in the press from disappointed or even angry visitors about non-working exhibits. What is exceptional about working exhibits in public environments is the demand for continuous unattended operation. This demand is more extreme than for commercial consumer products, and perhaps closer to features required for the military, for hospitals, and avionics. The need for durability, robustness, and low maintenance was not well understood outside the museum environment and this included the small companies that were typically contracted to make exhibits. It is also the case that museums, even large national museums, for the most part did not have the in-house technical expertise to specify exhibit design requirements to meet these demands. Working museum exhibits were mostly working prototypes and typically only one would be made. Their physical realisation did not have the benefit of generational development i.e. building and testing a series of prototypes and pre-production versions, each an improvement of the last, as would be the standard process for a consumer product. Non-working exhibits in public environments in the 1970s and 1980s suffered, quite justifiably, from bad press for poor reliability.

I believe that the success of Jack's company, *Museum Electronics*, was founded on two contributory factors. Firstly, Jack understood absolutely the need for reliability, robustness and low maintenance as essential features of working museum exhibits and had the technical expertise to ensure appropriate design and manufacture. Secondly, his interest and involvement coincided (astutely) with a new and rising global interest and market in science centres. Jack developed a range of working interactive exhibits that were 'catalogue products' that new science centres could select from. Making multiples of exhibits allowed him to build prototypes for development and to test the exhibits by the harsh needs of their future working environments. So a new science centre, which typically did not have the resources, technical or manufacturing, to produce exhibits in-house, could acquire off-the-shelf exhibits and in some cases, complete exhibitions.

At the time of my association with Jack I was Head of AVEC (Audio-visual, Electronic, and Computer-based Displays) at the Science Museum, London. The main challenge was to design and produce working exhibits to the highest achievable standards of reliability. A revolutionary gallery was the Telecommunications gallery that was opened by Prince Charles in 1983 for which we pioneered various techniques. Equipment for the whole gallery was, for the first time, centralised in a control room; each controller had automatic error detection and error monitoring; controllers automatically rebooted after each use by a visitor; all controllers booted automatically on switch-on without intervention by an operator. The most prolific controllers were for 'talking labels', i.e. an audio commentary available on demand to a visitor by lifting a handset or pressing a button. These were used widely in the Museum. The audio was recorded on magnetic tape and there were no commercial tape players with the requisite features of auto-starting, automatic fault detection, and durability. The only device we found that would suit was the MacKenzie 'message repeater' and Jack was the only source of supply I knew for these remarkable machines. Each machine had a bank of tape cartridges driven by the same capstan. They were superbly simple, hugely robust, bomb-proof and very expensive. We first equipped the Telecommunications Gallery with them, and subsequently, after proven success, elsewhere. I believe that Jack had chosen these machines because he profoundly understood the special demands made on device controllers for use in museum environments. He also had an astute sense of the value to science centres, and like organisations, of off - the - shelf exhibits – institutions that did not have the technical expertise to design or specify exhibits, or the maintenance staff to ensure continuity of service.

MacKenzie message repeaters are still made today though of course using solid - state technology rather than mechanical/electro-mechanical.

An exhibit that Jack supplied that was

particularly appealing for exhibition designers. Even though off-the-shelf exhibits were desirable for many reasons, and the science centres were in many different countries so duplication was not a significant issue, 'catalogue exhibits' did not have the caché of uniqueness that comes from customising them for specific subjects or specific institutions. One of the most successful of Jack's products was a generic question-answer exhibit involving multiple-choice questions that were answered by button presses. The point was that the customer could customise the display in-house for any subject i.e. could 'personalise' the questions and answers by doing no more than providing the text for the text panels. Correct answers were indicated by illuminated panel lights. These were very popular and allowed exhibitors to individualise a generic exhibit in any language.

Jack and the author's father-in-law Dr Leslie J Samuels MC at the AJEX parade November 1983.

Chapter Eighteen: The unsung hero

In the late 1980s an article appeared in the Daily Telegraph which was sharply critical of Lord Louis Mountbatten. My father-in-law, Dr. Leslie J. Samuels MC [Military Cross], saw the article and sent it to Jack in Toronto. He urged my father to write to the Telegraph with his view on how Mountbatten had been so instrumental in the success of the Combined Forces. His letter was published in Daily Telegraph.

Ken Dearson[17] was the redhead whom Jack later remembered had been in the room with Air Vice Marshall Victor Tait when Jack was given his orders for Dieppe. Quite by chance Ken was in the airport at Toronto, returning to England, and bought a copy of the Telegraph. He could not believe his eyes. All those years he and Mountbatten (whom he had worked with for many years after the war) had thought Jack had not returned from Dieppe. In those days of secrecy, it probably was not noted at the time that he had reported back, safe and relatively well.

Ken immediately asked the Telegraph for Jack's address in Canada, but they declined to give it, for reasons of privacy.

Ken, thinking Jack might well be a radio ham (amateur hobbyist) advertised in a radio ham society magazine in Canada. He asked if anyone knew the whereabouts of Jack Nissenthall. My parents said that for twenty-four hours their phone did not stop ringing.

Ken was back in touch with Jack after all those

---

[17] On the Imperial War Museum web site there are three audio tapes of an interview with Ken Dearson IWM 12548. From 9 minutes 50 seconds into the second file Ken talks about his and Jack's part in the Dieppe Raid, which carries on to the third file.

years. They corresponded, spoke frequently and eventually met. Ken began a campaign to gain a medal for Jack in recognition of his heroism at Dieppe and his services to radar in the Second World War. I was there in 1991 when they met at the World War II Radar Reunion in Coventry. Jack looked at the completely bald Ken, and said, "Where has all that red hair gone?" It was as if they only had met yesterday.

In his article, *Jack Nissenthall, the VC who never was,* Martin Sugarman, author and archivist for AJEX, the Jewish Ex-servicemen's Society wrote:

> In 1991 the first reunion of World War II radar personnel was held in Coventry. Jack Nissenthall was an honoured guest, but he did not even rate a mention in the souvenir programme which marked the event, and few even saw the presentation made to him – a replica of the precious Avometer his father gave him for his barmitzvah and that he lost in his toolkit on the Dieppe Raid.

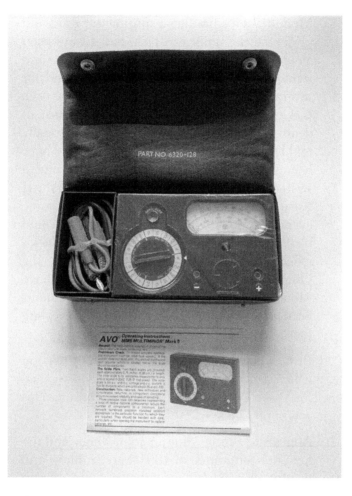

The Avometer presented to Jack by Ken Dearson at the Radar Reunion in Coventry in 1991 to replace the one bought by Jack's father as a Barmitzvah present for Jack, which Jack 'lost' on the Dieppe Raid.

Ken Dearson, who was a member of the

Mountbatten's briefing team for the Raid and presented the replica to Jack, had always been aware of his outstanding courage and remarkable achievement at Pourville, and for several years campaigned to get Jack the VC. Jack went to Dieppe 'under the sentence of death', he wrote. Mountbatten had personally told Dearson after the war that Jack should have been given a VC. But this means overturning a 1949 directive ending the issue of World War II gallantry medals. Dearson argues that some events, however, were so secret that little could be done about them till many years later. Jack's identity had been concealed for years by the Official Secrets Act, and only recently have Mountbatten's archives and other documents been released for public scrutiny, revealing Jack's crucial achievement.

In fact it was Mountbatten's publicity section which put out the story that a scientist called Professor Wendell had been on the Raid. This was in fact Jack.

Appeals to Prime Minister John Major and the honours committee in 1991 were fruitless, and to this day Jack Nissenthall's feats remain officially unrecognised. Jack spent his final years with Dell travelling between South Africa, England and Canada.

In 1991 Princess Diana and Prince Charles made an official visit to Canada. My father was invited to meet Prince Charles in Toronto and talk about his role in the Dieppe raid.

Jack at the fiftieth Dieppe Reunion proudly wearing the Dieppe Medal awarded by the Canadians for those who went on the Raid, together with his British service medals and campaign stars. From left to right; 1939-45 Star, North Africa Star, Italy Star, War Medal, Service Medal.

In 1992, on the fiftieth anniversary of the Dieppe Raid, HRH Prince Philip, The Duke of Edinburgh made a special request to meet my father in Lewes, where they were commemorating the event at the Town Hall. Our family went to the ceremony and later we then travelled from Newhaven to Dieppe for the Reunion.

It was in Canada, while supporting his brother Harold after his wife, Arlene's death, that Jack himself took ill, and died in Toronto.

He was buried on 11 November 1997 at the Pardes Shalom cemetery. A young army cadet saluted at the grave and members of the Canadian Jewish Ex-servicemen's Association attended in their marching attire, having first of all taken part in the Armistice Day Parade.

At 77 my father was relatively young, and until his illness, fit. My last memory of him in England was in June 1997 running upstairs with a large television!

Looking back on his life, I am sure he would say, that it had been exceedingly good.

After his death, Dell came to live for ten happy years in London. My brother Paul remained in South Africa and has a hotel in Boksburg, near Johannesburg, Elizabeth Lodge. Jack's grandchildren lead independent lives of their own. Paul's daughter Taryn lives in South Africa with her partner and our two are married with children of their own in London.

In the summer of 2019 we were away with our grandchildren visiting a theme park. Suddenly the six-year-old was speeding to the summit of a frighteningly high climbing net. Basil and I looked at each other, "I wonder where he gets that from?" he said.

In 1999, a plaque commemorating Jack was

unveiled at the end of the runway on the clifftop where the Bolt Head GCI Radar Station had been based. My mother Dell, her brother Max, his wife Marie (Jack's sister) and their families were there. Also Jack's brother Harold and his children from Canada attended, as did Henry Nisenthal our Argentinian second cousin and great-grandchild of Malka and Hersch Meyer[18]. The ceremony was arranged by Pam McNicoll, a WAAF who had worked with my father as a radar operator at Bolt Head. A flypast was arranged, including a Spitfire. It was a profoundly moving ceremony.

Dell, the author and other members of the family at the unveiling of the plaque erected at the site of the Bolt Head GCI radar station in 1999 on which are mentioned Jack's exploits on the Dieppe Raid.

[18] See Appendix 1

Dell, the author and others at the unveiling of the plaque at Bolt Head.

Unbeknown to me in 2012 two storytellers Umi Sinha and Elizabeth Scott were commissioned to perform a presentation for the 70th anniversary of the Dieppe raid. They chose Jack's story and have presented it several times. They also organized a collection for a memorial sculpture bench to be carved with his name[19].

There have been two unofficial tributes to Jack from His Royal Highness Prince Charles.

At the 250th anniversary of the British Board of Jewish Deputies Prince Charles gave a speech, thanking the Jewish Servicemen and women of both world wars.

He mentioned only one by name.

If I may, Ladies and Gentlemen, I just want to recall and recognize the fact that in two World Wars British Jews made an outstanding contribution to the defence of our values and of our liberty, on land, at sea and in the air. Many thousands were killed in action, on all the War fronts. Jews also volunteered to be parachuted behind enemy lines, and to serve on the most dangerous of missions. I know that my great uncle, Lord Mountbatten, was enormously proud of the Jewish airman, RAF Flight Sergeant Jack Nissenthall, a radar specialist. He knew that he would have to be shot by his own men if he was about to be captured, but he went ashore at Dieppe in 1942 to examine a crucial German radar station on the cliff top.

In December 2019, Prince Charles made another reference to Mountbatten's pride in Jack in a reception at Buckingham Palace to celebrate the Jewish Community in Britain.

A fitting tribute to an ordinary man blessed with extraordinary gifts and great heroism, my father.

---

[19] See Appendix 2

Jack's medals. British service medals and campaign stars. From left to right; 1939-45 Star, North Africa Star, Italy Star, War Medal, Service Medal.

Epilogue

What has amazed both my husband and me is how all the papers and documents we found when we began researching my father's life had survived. This was especially true of the letters that he had sent to his future wife, Dally. They had survived the Blitz in London, the move to their married home in Hayes, to South Africa where my parents had lived in various locations, to Toronto, where again they had had several homes and then finally back to England when my mother decided to return in 1998, and then to our house.

Why was Jack never decorated?

That is a question that has puzzled many people. Flight Sergeant Cox was awarded a Military Medal for his involvement on the Bruneval Raid carried out by paratroopers parachuted into northern France to investigate the Wurzburg Radar on the north French coast.

Operation Rutter the raid on Dieppe that was called off due to adverse weather conditions had been planned by Combined Operations under Mountbatten. He had raised serious concern over sending anyone with intimate knowledge of Britain's radar defences on the raid even though their expertise would have been invaluable. He was concerned that should the expert fall into enemy hands the Germans would gain insight into Britain's defences. However Air Vice Marshall Victor Tait, Director of RDF argued that only an expert could assess the new German Freya radar. It was for this reason and to assuage Mountbatten's concerns that included in the battle orders were instructions that the expert was to be accompanied by a bodyguard to ensure he didn't fall alive into the enemy's hands.

When Operation Rutter was called off, responsibility for its organisation as Operation Jubilee passed to Major-General J.H. Roberts, Commander of the 2nd Canadian Division, the commanding officer of the Canadian soldiers who were chosen to go.

Although he was aware that a British radar expert was to go with them on the raid, neither he nor any of the Canadian troops were given his name or to which service he belonged. Jack had no identity tags either.

Mountbatten was unaware that Jack had returned after the Raid and only discovered this in 1975. Did Air Vice Marshall Victor Tait withhold this from Mountbatten because of Mountbatten's misgivings and the fact that he had ignored Mountbatten, or was it because Mountbatten was no longer in charge? Maybe he thought the Canadian commanding officer would have passed that information on at the post Raid debriefing.

Why was a twenty-five-year D-Notice placed on Jack's participation? Was it to ensure as far as possible that the Germans would be unaware that the secrets of the Freya Radar and their Radar defence organisation had been revealed? Perhaps it was just as well that Jack was unable to get into the Freya station. If he had and bits of equipment and technical literature had been taken the Germans would have realised that the system had been compromised and they would have developed measures to ensure that it couldn't be disabled as it was so effectively on D-Day two years later.

Jack and Willi Weber. Willi was in charge of the radar defences at Pourville during the Dieppe Raid.

When Jack met Willi Weber at one of the Dieppe Raid reunions many years later they both discovered that just as the British Radar detection and plotting were so hush-hush that only personnel intimately involved were aware of the process, so it was with Germany. Although their radar had detected the approaching ships on that August day, he found it impossible to convince the Luftwaffe and Army personnel of his observation because he could not divulge anything about German radar. No visible sightings were possible because the craft were still some way offshore and it was dark!

Ken Dearson[20] who organised the campaign to get him a medal couldn't understand why he never received official recognition.

[20] Apart from the interview with Ken Dearson on the Imperial War Museum web site, there are five files of the interview with Jack Maurice Nissen, in which he recalls his involvement with radar and his part in the Dieppe Raid and what was learned about German radar. IWM Oral History 10762.

Appendix 1 – Fate of Jack's family in Poland

What Jack couldn't know was that in 1942 his paternal grandparents would be brutally murdered by the Nazis in their Polish village. Annopol (Rachow) was where Aaron Nissenthall, Jack's father, was born on 28 February 1895. He was one of nine children. Life was hard there, with violent pogroms, constant bullying, and to avoid the draft many young men would leave at an early age, or (more drastically) elect to have part of their trigger finger surgically removed. The town Aaron came from was on the banks of the Vistula River. Aaron's father, Hersch Myer, who possessed a very large cart, was the local taxi driver. Mick Bryk, whom my husband and I met in London in the nineties, had been a friend of the family, and said they were 'well off' because most other houses had dirt floors, but Hersch Myer's house had a wooden floor.

Because of the grinding poverty and endless harassment, Hersch Myer was keen to get as many of his children out of Poland as possible. Two went to Argentina, one to Brazil and two to England. His eldest son, Ziesel owned a wood mill, and according to his cousin, Esther Nisenthal Krinitz (whom my husband and I knew), he was sent to Dachau in 1939, and his ashes were sent back to the family in an urn. Sadly the rest of the family who stayed in Poland perished with their families in the camps.

In September 1942 all the Jews of Annopol were ordered to go to Krasnik railway station. Hersch Myer refused to go to the railway station, as he and his invalid wife Malka were too old. The Germans made him dig a grave in the front garden of their house, and then his invalid wife was dragged from her sickbed, placed in the grave and was shot. Hersch Myer was forced to fill the grave. According to reports, his wailing voice while reciting the Kaddish (Jewish mourner's prayer) could be heard throughout the neighbourhood. He was then rounded up with the remaining Jews, taken out of the town to a forest where they too met their deaths at the end of a gun. This witness account is from the "Yiskor" memorial book, especially written for the town of Annopol by the few survivors.

(Translation from the Yiddish made by Jennifer Bell and Diane Levitin.)

Photograph of Jack's uncle Max Nissenthall, holding the reins of Hersch Myer's cart in Annopol, Poland in 1936. In the cart are Hersch Myer sitting at the back with the long beard, Ziesel Nissenthall next to him, Golda Nissenthall's father-in-law, Golda and her husband Zelig, Hersch Myer's nephew Chiel Kestenbaum, Max and Celia Nissenthall. Apart from Max and Celia, they all perished in 1942.

Appendix 2 – Umi Sinha and Elizabeth Scott

Early in 2018, I received an amazing email. It was from Umi Sinha, who with Elizabeth Scott, has been telling my father's heroic story since 2012, the 70th Anniversary of the Dieppe Raid.

It was only this year that they managed to locate me through the wonders of the web. Not only did I discover that they had been telling my dad's story (very poignant for me) but also that they had organised, through donations, for my dad's name to be carved on a memorial sculpture bench overlooking the sea from Newhaven to Dieppe.

Umi Sinha writes:

In 2012 I was commissioned by Sara Clifford, who was putting on an Arts Council project to commemorate the 70th anniversary of the Dieppe Raid, to create a performance about the Raid.

Elizabeth Scott and I gave our one hour storytelling performance of 'The Freya Connection' in Pourville, near Dieppe. Set in 1942, it relates the story of one man's part in the Dieppe Raid.

Our story concerns Jack Nissenthall, a 24 year old radar expert and Cockney of Polish Jewish extraction, who volunteered to break into the heavily guarded radar station at Pourville to assess the capabilities of German Freya radar. Because of his knowledge of top secret British radar systems, he had to agree to allow himself to be killed by his own bodyguards if he was in danger of falling into enemy hands.

The Raid, which was launched from the south coast of England, was a practice run for the planned invasion, and a military disaster. It lasted less than a day, and two-thirds of the six thousand soldiers, mostly Canadians, who landed on the beaches of northern France, were either captured or killed. It is generally regarded as a complete failure.

The story was meant to be a one off performance for the anniversary, but the way it was received convinced Elizabeth and me that we should go on telling it. We felt it was important for people to hear it because Jack received no recognition for his heroic part in the Raid, and routinely encountered anti-Semitism, even from those with whom he was serving.

Both my father and Elizabeth's father and uncle served in the Second World War, and we include some brief anecdotes about them that may partly explain why we both feel such a strong connection to Jack's story.

Appendix 3 – Creating Canada

A few weeks after I completed the first draft of this biography, I was surprised and delighted to hear from Michael Nissenthal, Harold's son. (Harold was my father's much younger brother)

Michael's daughter was at school in Toronto, Canada.

He writes:

My daughter's grade 10 history class text book has a page on Jack.

How amazing is that! Schools in Canada are teaching kids about him.

Dennis Burton who lives in Buenos Aires sent me the following observation:-

This is absolutely fascinating and heart-warming. Thank you very much for sending this on. I can see exactly why your friend is so proud of her father and why she is frustrated that he has not received recognition. But this seems to me to be recognition beyond all compare. What can be better than being included in a textbook – I assume for school children – as an example of a key person who may have helped avoid defeat in the Second World War. This to me seems a much greater compliment than some award by the Queen, which will be forgotten as soon as it is collected, if not before. This is already going down in history, being put forward as an example to young children who will remember you and be inspired by your example. Goodness, it doesn't get a lot better than this.

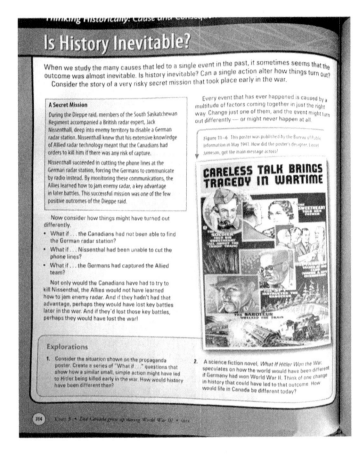

Page from Creating Canada, in which the story of Jack's participation in the Dieppe Raid is used in the Standard 10 Curriculum in Ontario, Canada.

The text reads as follows:

Is History Inevitable?

When we study the many causes that led to a single event in the past, it sometimes seems that the outcome was almost inevitable. Is history inevitable? Can a single action alter how things turn out? Consider the story of a very risky secret mission that took place early in the war.

Every event that has ever happened is caused by a multitude of factors coming together in just the right way. Change one of them, and the event might turn out differently – or might never happen at all.

A Secret Mission

During the Dieppe raid, members of the South Saskatchewan Regiment accompanied a British radar expert, Jack Nissenthall, deep into enemy territory to disable a German radar station. Nissenthall knew that his extensive knowledge of Allied radar technology meant that the Canadians had orders to kill him if there was any risk of capture.

Nissenthall succeeded in cutting the phone lines at the German radar station, forcing the Germans to communicate by radio instead. By monitoring these communications, the Allies learned how to jam enemy radar, a key advantage in later battles. This successful mission was one of the few positive outcomes of the Dieppe raid.

Now consider how things might have turned out differently:

- What if… the Canadians had not been able to find the German radar station?

- What if… Nissenthall had been unable to cut the phone lines?

- What if… the Germans had captured the allied team?

Not only would the Canadians have had to try and kill Nissenthall, the Allies would not have learned how to jam enemy radar. And if they hadn't had that advantage, perhaps they would have lost key battles later in the war. And if they'd lost those key battles, perhaps they would have lost the war.

Jack's gravestone at Pardes Shalom cemetery, 10953 Dufferin St, Maple, Ontario, Canada

Bibliography

There are many books and articles written about Radar and the Dieppe Raid, far too many to list here, but these have been the most pertinent.

Green Beach, James Leasor, Heinemann 1975

Winning the Radar War, A W Cockerill, Macmillan of Canada 1987

Britain's Shield: Radar and the Defeat of the Luftwaffe, David Zimmerman, Amberley Publishing; Reprint Edition (15 Aug. 2010)

Second World War, Martin Gilbert, George Weidenfeld and Nicolson Ltd 1989

Fighting Back, Martin Sugarman, Valentine Mitchell 2010

The Invention That Changed The World, Robert Buderi, Abacus 1998

Dress Rehearsal, Quentin Reynolds, Random House 1943

Creating Canada, Jill Colyer, Jack Cecillon, McGraw-Hill Ryerson 2014

Suggested further reading

Bawdsey: Birth of the Beam, Gordon Kinsey, Terence Dalton Limited 1983

Radar Days, E G Bowen, Adam Higler 1987

Three Steps to Victory, Robert Watson-Watt, Odham's Press Limited 1957

Combined Operations, The Macmillan Company, New York 1943

Most Secret War, R V Jones, Hamish Hamilton London   1978

John Hearfield's 2012 essay 'Chain Home and the Cavity Magnetron' about the birth and development of radar
is to be found on this webpage:
http://www.johnhearfield.com/Radar/Magnetron.htm

This easily understood explanation of quite a complex subject is well worth reading.

Glossary

AI   Air-Interception Radar. A radar installation in night fighters for direction and interception of enemy aircraft.

AJEX   Association of Jewish Ex Servicemen and Servicewomen.

AMES Air Ministry Experimental Station. This acronym was applied initially to Bawdsey, which was AMES 1, but later referred to all the radar systems and also to radar stations abroad, and is still in use today.

ASV   Air to Surface Vessel. An airborne radar for detection of ships and surfaced submarines

CH   Chain Home. The first chain of air-warning radar along the east and south coasts of Britain to provide early warning of the approach of enemy aircraft.

CHL   Chain Home Low. A network added later to supplement Chain Home by giving warning of low-flying aircraft.

GCI   Ground Controlled Interception Radar. A ground-based radar for the control of fighters equipped with AI.

GEE   A medium-range hyperbolic radio navigation system used by bomber command.

IFF   A radar device for Identification of Friend from Foe. Aeroplanes fitted with this would transmit a signal on the same frequency as the radar and it would appear as a brighter 'blob' on the cathode ray tube which the operator would recognise.

LAC   Leading Aircraftman. A junior rank in some air forces. It sits between aircraftman and senior aircraftman. Leading Aircraftmen and women would have done everything from maintain aircraft to cooking and basic clerical tasks.

LCA   Landing Craft Assault. Its primary purpose was to ferry troops from transport ships to attack enemy-held shores.

NCO Non-Commissioned Officer

OBOE A highly accurate blind bombing aid used by RAF Pathfinder Squadrons.

PPI   Plan Position Indicator.

RDF   The early name for radar in Britain - Radio Detection Finding

TRE Telecommunications Research Establishment

About the Author

Linda Nissen Samuels, Jack Nissenthall's daughter, was born and educated in South Africa. The author lives with her husband in London and is an artist and teacher. Her African landscape images used by WaterAid as their annual greeting cards proved extremely popular worldwide raising substantial funds for that charity.

An award-winning short-story writer, she has also published several children's books. Her how to draw book, Draw Water and Other Things, has proved extremely popular. Its sequel Draw Queens, Kings and All Things Royal has been on sale at The Royal Collection. In addition, she has published a series for children on climate change, which have been endorsed by Sir David Attenborough and Dr Sylvia Earle (director of Mission Blue USA).

Linda Nissen Samuels is uniquely qualified to write this book, having known Jack for half a century!

Printed in Great Britain
by Amazon

12992378R00195